THE
SUCCESSFUL
LAWYER

Powerful Strategies for
Transforming Your Practice

Gerald A. Riskin

LAW PRACTICE MANAGEMENT SECTION
MARKETING • MANAGEMENT • TECHNOLOGY • FINANCE

Commitment to Quality: The Law Practice Management Section is committed to quality in our publications. Our authors are experienced practitioners in their fields. Prior to publication, the contents of all our books are rigorously reviewed by experts to ensure the highest quality product and presentation. Because we are committed to serving our readers' needs, we welcome your feedback on how we can improve future editions of this book.

Cover design by Dan Mazanec, ABA Publishing.

Cover photo by Kirk Russell (www.russellstudiophoto.com).

Library of Congress Cataloging-in-Publication Data
The Successful Lawyer: Powerful Strategies for Transforming Your Practice. Gerald A. Riskin: Library of Congress Cataloging-in-Publication Data is on file.

ISBN 1-59031-534-0

09 08 07 06   5 4 3 2

Discounts are available for books ordered in bulk. Special consideration is given to state bars, CLE programs, and other bar-related organizations. Inquire at Book Publishing, American Bar Association, 321 N. Clark Street, Chicago, Illinois 60610.

Contents

PART IV
INCREASING YOUR VALUE   103

PART V
THE BUSINESS SIDE OF LAW   155

About the Author

Gerald A. Riskin

Gerald A. Riskin, B.Comm., L.L.B., is a Canadian lawyer and business graduate with a global reputation as an author, management consultant and pioneer in the field of professional-firm economics and marketing. He is a Visiting Fellow of The College of Law in London and a Visiting Professor to the Gordon Institute of Business Science at the University or Pretoria in South Africa. He has served the Conference Board of Canada, and recently he was keynote speaker at a World Masters of Law Firm Management conference in Sydney, Australia.

A popular facilitator, teacher and retreat speaker, he has been described by *The Financial Post* as "Canada's professional firm management and marketing guru, with a client base stretching from Britain to the United States." Professional marketing pioneer Bruce Marcus has said of him that he is "light years ahead of almost everybody else," and the head of a national conference recently described his session as "the best practice-related seminar [I have] ever attended."

After graduating from the University of Alberta with a Bachelor of Commerce (with Distinction) and a Bachelor of Laws, Gerry practiced law for ten years with two major Edmonton firms—becoming a partner of the first in 1979, and serving the second, which had offices in Hong Kong as well as Canada, as managing partner. Gerry was consistently one of the top three rainmakers in his firm, and he quickly began to develop a reputation which led to a demand for him to teach others to do the same.

In 1983, with Patrick McKenna, Gerry Riskin co-founded The Edge Group. He remains a principal partner with the company, which evolved to become Edge International in 2001. According to a recent survey by *Of Counsel* in the U.S., Edge International is now the most popular marketing consultancy to major U.S. law firms. The company is truly global, with active clients in Canada, the USA, the UK, Europe, CIS (formerly Russia), Australia, the Far East, South Africa and elsewhere—more than 30 countries in all.

Today, Gerry's private clients include the most prominent professional-service firms in the world, and he has provided them with assistance in such areas as marketing, strategic planning, one-on-one coaching, merging, multi-office management, practice-group and industry-group management, client-relations skills training, and management training. In addition to his work with private firms, he has spoken at meetings of the Canadian Bar Association, the American Bar Association, the American Institute of Certified Public Accountants, the Law Society of the UK, the Institute of Law Firm Management (LMA), Centaur Conferences (UK), the National Association of Law Firm Marketing Administrators, and numerous other organizations all over the world.

In 1989, at the invitation of the major international legal publishing firm Butterworths, Gerry coauthored a text on the marketing of legal services entitled *Practice Development: Creating the Marketing Mindset*. This book was recognized in 1995 by an international journal as "one of the top ten books that any professional services marketer should have on their bookcase." He has also co-written two books for practitioners with management responsibilities, *Herding Cats* and *Beyond Knowing*, both of which became management bestsellers. Gerry is also the co-creator of the acclaimed learning systems Practice-Coach® and Rainmaking®, as well as the six-CD audio Successful Lawyer® program.

Gerry Riskin lives in the British West Indies.

Acknowledgments

For thirty years, I have served lawyers around the world as a consultant. I am typically hired by big firms, and I deal with their senior-management teams. I have had the good fortune of training and counseling the most promising performers in the world of law.

One day as my wife Bethany and I were relaxing on the veranda of a quaint cottage just off the Great Ocean Road in Australia, watching waterfowl on a small lake, I told her my dream of sharing with individual lawyers—whether senior or junior, and whether in the largest or the smallest firms in the world—the lessons I had learned in the course of my career. I explained that I wanted to deliver the knowledge I had gained to those who might otherwise have no access to someone doing work like mine.

From that moment on, Bethany was my encourager, catalyst and constructive critic. She patiently brainstormed the topic list with me, challenged my assumptions, and made me dig deeper to prove my assertions with illustrations. Then she used her own experience as a stage performer and software-company marketing manager to guide me through the recording of the six-disk audio program entitled *The Successful Lawyer* which preceded this book. Bethany, bless you—I can never thank you enough.

Thank you also to my editor, Mary W. Walters, who helped transform a transcript of that audio program into a literary endeavor. If you like this work, a lot of credit goes to Mary. As a published author in her own right, Mary understands things about composition and structure that I will never know. You, as reader, are also a beneficiary of her knowledge. Thank you, Mary.

Thank you also to Beverly Loder, Director of LPM Publishing, who leads the publishing team at the American Bar Association; she has been wonderful in giving me guidance and keeping me out of the publishing sand traps. Thank you also to Neal Cox, Director, LPM Publishing Marketing Planning & Promotion at the ABA, who has been flexible and encouraging throughout the book-design process. Thank you to lawyer Stephen P. Gallagher, who read this manuscript as a member of the ABA's editorial board, for his encouragement and ideas.

The photograph on the cover of this book was a gift to me from world-famous photographer Kirk Russell, whose portfolio includes a spectrum of subjects, including a United States president, Fortune Top Ten executives who send private jets to fetch him, the jets themselves, fabulously exotic luxury yachts, and landscapes of the loveliest and most beautiful places in the world. One of these is the island upon which Kirk, his wife Beverley, and Bethany and I reside, Anguilla, British West Indies. Thank you Kirk, for the beautiful image and the inspiration to use it.

I consider myself very fortunate to have had the opportunity to work for several years with David Maister, former Harvard Business School professor and prolific writer. David is revered by professional firm leaders for the strength of his intelligence and creativity, which combine to form enormously effective catalysts for thought and leadership. Thank you so much, David, for your input on this manuscript, and for writing the foreword to the book.

I am also extremely grateful to: Larry Smith of Levick Strategic, whose talents transcend his brilliant contributions to legal journalism and crisis management; Bruce Marcus, a prolific author and ideas generator whose way of seeing the world offers insights that have been powerful tools in my kit for so many years; my friends Larry Anderson, a co-founder of Lincolnberg Homes and many other successful businesses, a genius at managing and motivating, a role model to many and a legend in his community for his outstanding philanthropy; Phil Milroy, a world-class developer who remains the person he has always been—totally genuine, without pretense, David Kirk (1947–2005) and Louis Gratton, whose life-long friendship and encouragement to dare to do the unusual have meant so much to me. All of these individuals and their spouses are friends of Bethany's and mine, providing support while also challenging us to continue to set new goals.

Thanks also to my "dream team" at Edge International. I met my co-founder Patrick McKenna when as the vice president of a publicly traded company, he was appointed to the board of a pharmaceutical distribution company which was my largest client. Patrick and I created the client-relations-skills program called Rainmaking®, a truly synergistic act that combined his knowledge of the training process with my experience as a practicing lawyer in an establishment firm. Subsequently, over 300 law firms around the globe experienced that program, including the-then largest law firm in the world. Over the years, other people have joined us at Edge International to breathe life into our vision of helping the legal profession by enhancing its members' practice satisfaction by helping them better serve their clients. Many thanks to Patrick and his wife, Monique, and to the other members of our geographically scattered but always cohesive team: Ed Wesemann (Savannah, GA), Nick Jarrett-Kerr (Bristol, U.K.), Karen MacKay (Toronto, ON), Robert Millard (Johannesburg, South Africa), Michael Anderson (Vancouver, B.C.), and Friedrich Blasé (Frankfurt, Germany). Our dream team also includes Christine Birdseye, who was for so many years the glue that held our virtual organization together.

Thank you also to Sue Stapely of London, a lawyer and reputational-management expert, for inviting me to present in the U.K. and Brussels and then for collaborating with me: you have been a true friend and confidante. Thanks also to Merrilyn Tarlton, consultant and editor of the ABA's *Law Practice* magazine, who has always been supportive and encouraging.

There is a very long list of people to whom I am bound by my sense of propriety not to name individually, but am free to mention in the aggregate. Thank you to my clients over the better part of twenty years in my practice of law: you were demanding and appreciative and taught me so much about how my practice could be fine-tuned to enhance your satisfaction. Thank you to the lawyers and staff with whom I practiced, beginning at Emery Jamieson—a firm unsurpassed in its passion for quality and sense of honor and integrity, with a dream list of clients attracted by founders who mastered the art of business development. Later, the lawyers and staff at Snyder & Co. were entrepreneurial enough to bring me on board as managing partner. They allowed me to test my theories and beliefs about the management of a firm, and taught me with affection and respect how I might constantly improve methodologies to make them more practical and effective "in the real world." Thank you also to the lawyers and staff at Keithley Lake & Associates in Anguilla for giving me a professional home, and for your friendship and support. And many thanks to all of my Edge clients, who entrust me with assignments that range from skills enhancement to governance, strategic management and marketing.

I thank my Dad and Mom, may they both rest in peace, for providing such outstanding role models throughout Dad's 55-year dental practice (with Mom acting as manager, because she wanted to). By exhibiting such deep caring and affection for those they served, they showed me how professionals can provide superior service to their clients. Patients laughed in their office, and they cried when Dad retired. I hope that this book begins to reflect some of the lessons my parents taught me.

To my brother, Robert, who lives with his wife, Trish, in Vancouver, I extend thanks not only for continuing moral support, but for being the genius at television production that you are, and for making world-class video productions for Edge International over the years.

Finally, I thank my phenomenal kids—Daniel, Matthew, and Raquel—for their zest for life, unwavering commitments to what they wish to achieve, and their diverse senses of humor. They remind me constantly that life is to be enjoyed as well as mastered. My wonderful children, you compel me to continue to be the best I can be every day—and perhaps to be even better tomorrow.

Gerry Riskin

Foreword

Gerry Riskin is a practical man, and this is an eminently practical book. It is stuffed with good advice, but more importantly it is advice that is presented in a manner that is easily absorbed and easily implemented.

Most of us know more than we put into practice, and that is the key contribution of this book. It does not set out to impress the reader with blinding insights or intricate theories (although it does contain some of each). It sets out to help the reader by pointing out actions that can be taken tomorrow (or today), actions that will lead to both a quick payoff and a lasting improvement.

Gerry has discussed these ideas with lawyers around the world. They are road-tested, and can be shown to have produced benefits wherever they have been applied.

The path to improvement must begin somewhere, and for lawyers who wish to be truly successful, that starting place is here.

David H. Maister
Author and Consultant

Introduction

Are *You* Where You Want to Be?

Some years ago an American Bar Association committee looked into the satisfaction levels of practicing lawyers, and the findings of this committee were extraordinary. They indicated that as many as 70 percent of lawyers would prefer to be doing something else if they could still make a decent living.

What does that tell us?

It tells us that we have some pretty unhappy people in our profession.

When we get out of bed in the morning and we think about working as lawyers, we should feel enthusiastic. If we are not feeling enthusiastic, we need to do something about it. We need to steer our practice in the direction of work we enjoy, and toward serving people with whom we want to work.

"Impossible," you may say. "That's too idealistic. You just don't understand." You can probably give me convincing reasons why my suggestion cannot work in your particular situation—perhaps reasons like the following:

- "My market is limited."
- "I'm in a large firm and I have to do what I'm told to do."
- "I'm very junior and I'm paying my dues."
- "I have been practicing for many years and I don't have the skills to change focus at this stage of my career."

In the hundreds and hundreds of seminars and workshop presentations I have made to lawyers, I have heard all of those reasons—and many, many others.

Let us suspend all those excuses for a moment. Let us look instead at a related question:

Do you believe that you have any control over your destiny at all? Yes or no?

Most readers will likely agree that we do have some control over our destiny—if we didn't, we probably would not have chosen the profession that we have. And if we do have some control over our destiny, then I contend that we ought to be using some of that control to steer our careers in directions we find exciting, in directions that we find stimulating, in directions that are going to give us the natural enthusiasm and the natural passion to practice law in the way law *ought* to be practiced—for the sake of our clients as well as ourselves.

Some people believe that exciting and fulfilling practices are reserved for a few gifted, extraordinary people who somehow magically rise to the top. After watching some of the best professionals in the world over the last number of years, I can tell you that this simply is not true. It is my observation that the people who have the most fulfilling and exciting practices are the people who have *intended* to do so. Stimulating and rewarding practices are the result of premeditated acts on the part of certain lawyers.

Getting Started

I invite you to join those lawyers who have decided to control their destinies. In this book, you will encounter ideas, examples, and anecdotes that come from the best practices of some of the most successful lawyers in the world. With this information available for your use, the choices become yours. Which aspects will you adopt into your own life? Which pieces or parts will you find valuable enough and appropriate enough to apply to your particular practice?

A lot of people in this world are very good at assimilating information, but not so good at taking action based on that information. People like that would be better off passing this book to someone else immediately, because it will be of no benefit to them. If you want to benefit from the contents of this book and by doing so achieve new levels of satisfaction as a lawyer, you need to make a promise to yourself right now. The promise is very simple. You need to promise yourself that as you read, you will be on the lookout for ideas that will help you improve your situation.

You are allowed to be discerning. You are allowed to be discriminating. You are allowed to be *very* careful regarding what actions you adopt for yourself. However, adopting a winning attitude means *looking* for those few ideas that you think will enhance *your* practice, will enhance *your* satisfaction, will enhance the success *you* experience as a lawyer.

I recommend that you start a journal or, if you prefer, a notebook (they are really very similar as I describe them, and I will use the terms interchangeably throughout this book). Whatever you use, leave lots of space for inserting additional ideas in the future. Also, I suggest that you reserve the first couple of pages of your notebook for an index that you can create as you move forward. Simply number your pages in sequence, and reference in your index what is on each page or page group. Throughout this book, I will prompt you from time to time in places where you may wish to capture your own ideas and information in your journal, but you should use it whether prompted or not whenever you get an insight or think of a worthwhile action. The investment of time in keeping a journal will turbo-charge the benefits you get from this book.

I highly recommend that you start keeping track of the ideas that appeal to you right now. Don't miss a single one. You may never get around to reading *The Successful Lawyer* again—most of us have better things to do than repeat the same learning processes—so take full advantage of your first time through. Underline meaningful passages, jot notes in the margins, record thoughts in your notebook. Be discriminating, yes, but capture those suggestions that you think make sense for *you*. Do not let them get away.

A Bit At a Time

In the previous section I said, "Adopting a winning attitude means looking for those few ideas that will help you improve your situation." Notice that word "few."

There is a lot of content later in this book that is related to taking action, but let me give you my first observation about successful professionals right now: Winners don't overdo it. Winners don't take on long "to-do" lists and then let themselves get demoralized. They don't end up having to say to themselves, "Here I go again. In a moment of euphoria and enthusiasm I decided on a hundred things I could do to improve my life. Since then I have addressed absolutely none of the ideas on my list and I'm more dejected than I was before I started. It was all just motivational garbage."

The materials you find within this book will not end up in the motivational garbage bin if you, like other winners, decide, "No, I won't take on a hundred ideas. I won't take on ninety-eight ideas. I'll take on one or two or three. If and when I choose to take on more, it will be over a time period during which I can reasonably expect to be able to implement them."

A Two-Percent Solution

As lawyers, we are highly cerebral people. In fact, studies by researchers outside the legal profession have shown that we grasp concepts faster than any other identifiable group in society. This is good news: we have no aversion to information and we assimilate it quickly. Unfortunately, some of us have assimilated so much information and grasped so many concepts, we think we have seen it all. How often have you walked out of a seminar and heard someone say, "It's good to know there's nothing new that I have to worry about. I knew all that before I went in!"?

This is a losing attitude. Winners (in all walks of life—sports, politics, you name it, as well as the professions) do not have that attitude. They do not look for the 98 percent of the content of a seminar that they knew already, and walk out complacent that there is nothing new. They look for the 2 percent they *did not* know and then they figure out "Is that worthwhile information for me to have?"

And if they say, "Yes, it is worthwhile," then they do the magical thing. They act on it. They actually implement it.

Learning From the Winners

My career to date includes almost twenty years as a practicing lawyer, including several years as the managing partner of a law firm with offices in both Canada and Hong Kong. As a co-founder and partner in the Edge Group, now Edge International, I have had the opportunity over the past number of years of consulting to professionals involved in a range of traditional practices in disciplines including the law, accounting, engineering, architecture, and others, not to mention individuals working in more unusual settings that included a government, an army, and a railway. The opportunities these experiences have given me to observe and reflect on professional "best practices" have led me to write this book. The program it contains was not designed to tell you what to do. It was not designed to give you a menu that you must follow slavishly or by rote. It respects the knowledge and experience you have acquired on your own, particularly when it comes to your own individual practice.

What this program was designed to do is to offer *catalysts* for your consideration. It is intended to give you *alternatives* that you may not have thought of on your own. It was created to save you a lot of heartache and even a few mistakes by allowing you to find out what others have done that has worked successfully for them.

Trust Your Own Judgment

In your daily life, you must take into consideration the views of many other people, not only those with whom you work, but also those with whom you live. In such situations, it becomes second nature for most people—especially lawyers, who are usually trying to eliminate problems before they arise—to consult. However, in order to build the kind of practice that will offer you the future that *you* want, many of the choices you need to make will be very personal.

Consider this program a personal companion—a personal source of information, ideas, even inspiration. At some point you will likely need and want to share at least some of your conclusions with others, but it is highly recommended that you first deliberate about the ideas in this program, and come to your conclusions on your own.

Go with your own instincts in this program. *You* will make the best choices for you.

Program Objectives

The Successful Lawyer program is intended to help you become a more efficient lawyer. It is intended to help you have a more effective practice. And it is intended to help you derive great satisfaction from your professional career.

Think about the words "efficient" and "effective." "Efficient" means doing things well; "effective" means doing the right things. How often do we find ourselves doing the right things, but not very efficiently? That doesn't get us very far. Conversely, how often do we work on less productive things extremely well? We don't get too far that way either. Extraordinary achievers exhibit the discipline to refrain from spending time on the chaff, so that they do not deplete the precious resources of time and energy they require to attend to the wheat.

Some of the chaff is quite seductive. It might afford immediate gratification (I'll just answer this unimportant e-mail right now) or it may be fun (I'll design the new letterhead myself—it's kind of neat to see what I can do with this software). Being *effective* really requires that you learn the art of saying "No" (described in more detail in Chapter 47, "The Power of Saying No"). Being *efficient* means learning how to do what must be done with quality, but with the expenditure of the lowest possible amount of your resources. Having effective tools and templates and utilizing technology means less time and effort are expended on each matter. The people who accomplish a great deal—the winners—somehow manage to do the most important things (they are effective) in the best possible way (they are efficient). It is the aim of this book to empower you to do the same.

Now, let us think about the "satisfaction" part of the equation. A "satisfying professional career" means a practice that you enjoy, a practice that you find fun as well as profitable. A satisfying career returns the financial rewards that are commensurate with the value you give to your clients, but also offers you satisfaction on a personal level. It allows you to focus on those kinds of legal matters that you *want* to do. It allows you to put your particular skills and expertise to work. It allows you to work with industries that you enjoy working with and—perhaps most importantly—it allows you to serve clients you enjoy.

Lawyers who find a way to work effectively and efficiently, who serve clients they enjoy, who do work they like to do in industries that fascinate them, are lawyers who improve their value to others while also experiencing happy and fulfilling careers. The best lawyers in the world have acquired skills and developed methodologies that we can all put to use to make our practices more personally and professionally rewarding for ourselves, while also increasing our value to those for whom—and with whom—we work.

An Overview of The Successful Lawyer Program

The Successful Lawyer program is going to give you the elements that will assist you to develop a better practice. You are going to look at how you can become more valuable as a practicing lawyer—more valuable to your firm, more valuable to your clients, and more valuable to yourself.

You will learn how to develop the kind of practice that you want to have. You will learn effective strategies that will help you to steer your practice in the direction you want it to go. You will see how you can design for yourself the kind of clientele you want to have.

You are going to learn certain very specific skills that are relevant to the kind of practice you would like to have—and you will learn how to acquire them quickly. In the client relations area for example, you will learn one-on-one skills that will increase your impact, help you enhance the satisfaction level of existing clients, and help you to attract prospective clients at will.

During the course of this book, we will also look at some other issues that affect you in your work, and talk about how to overcome some of the pressures that you face. These are some examples of issues that are examined in this book:

- How to be a better leader in situations where you need to offer leadership.
- How to combat the pressures of time. There is never enough time in the law firm environment, but you will learn how to use the time you have far more effectively.
- How to make meetings more productive, and much more appealing to those who have to attend them.
- How to have a more effective law practice from a financial perspective. This area includes reducing costs of practice so that you can increase margins and have more profitability, examining how you bill, and looking at how you manage the finances—all with the view to gaining higher client satisfaction and a more successful practice.

The Nature of the Beast: Why Lawyers May Find It Difficult to Make Improvements to Their Practices

In order to create and entertain ideas that will make their practices more satisfying and successful, most lawyers will need to train themselves to temporarily put aside certain skills and attributes that are, in fact, typical of members of our profession and even essential to it.

A few years ago my partner in Edge International, Patrick McKenna, and I published a book called *Herding Cats* on the subject of law-office management. For the cover we selected the fiercest-looking photograph of a lion we could find. This image was intended to convey our conviction that lawyers are the most ferociously independent people on this planet who have ever chosen to work in groups. In fact, many lawyers chose to practice law in the first place because they wanted a lot of control: they wanted to be able to decide for themselves how they would conduct their work, and how they would serve their clients. They wanted the freedom to be independent thinkers.

In addition to being ferociously independent, lawyers are also highly critical and analytical. These attributes are absolutely essential for good lawyering. When you review a legal document, you are looking for any amendment that can be made to that document that will make it more effective. At the top of your game, you are also looking for omissions—concepts that ought to have been addressed in that document that were not.

If you are a litigator and you are used to having opposing counsel, then you are accustomed to listening to arguments with a view to destroying them—no matter how excellent they are. Not only are you thinking about how to destroy them, you are also thinking in what sequence to destroy them for the best strategic impact. As lawyers, we tend constantly to be doing simultaneous translations of everything we see and hear in a highly critical and analytical way. These skills may be essential to good lawyering, but they can interfere with other aspects of our lives—as our "significant others" frequently remind us when we are being analytical and critical with them. We all need to be able to suspend those skills when appropriate—and one of those times is when we are being innovative and creative regarding the future of our practices. Being critical and analytical are different mental processes from being innovative and creative, and the human brain will not allow us to do both at the same time.

The third relevant propensity we have as lawyers is to be rather tense. Too often we take the mental posture of firefighters in the midst of a dangerous blaze, anticipating unexpected chemical explosions. Firefighters in such situations are not ideally positioned for receiving and implementing suggestions as to how to improve their skills and make their lives more rewarding. We need to be more relaxed to entertain new ideas.

So, as lawyers we are ferociously independent, we are critical and analytical, and we are tense. What this combination can add up to is very low receptivity to some of the information that can help us most. We need to think about this tendency not only for ourselves but also for the other lawyers with whom we practice. Such mind-sets can result in very limiting behaviors. During the course of this program you will find a significant number of specific examples of how you can employ tactics, inside your firm and outside your firm, in your professional life, and in your personal life, that will help you overcome—or at least neutralize—these propensities when necessary.

The "Slight Edge" Theory

A number of years ago, one of my best clients invited me to attend a seminar with him. This client is extraordinary—a winner by any definition. He started as a residential realtor but soon graduated into more complex development work, and he discovered how to become valuable to financial institutions during a recession by managing properties that were taken back in foreclosures. He has been enormously successful in many areas. He's created software. He's created systems. He flies his own jet. He has been phenomenal in his field.

The seminar I attended with him focused on a concept called the "Slight Edge Theory." This theory has had a tremendous impact on my thinking and on the thinking of those with whom I have worked over the last number of years. (In fact, if you notice a similarity between the name of the theory and the name of our company, Edge International, you are making an accurate connection.) I think the Slight Edge Theory may have a big impact on your thinking, too, especially in terms of how you can implement and act upon the suggestions contained within this book.

The Slight Edge theory is actually quite simple. Think of a golf tournament involving 72 holes, which Tiger Woods wins with a score of 281. Now think about the player who comes in second. What is his score? 282 perhaps? Determination of the winner may actually come down to a play-off round between Woods and this person who ends up in second place. So what is the percentage difference between the performance of Tiger Woods and the second-place finisher? A third of a percent, perhaps—an almost inconsequential amount. A "slight edge" is all.

Yet look at the first-place prize as compared to the second-place prize. The first-place prize might be millions, and the second-place prize is . . . well, far, far less. Similar outcomes occur in other competitive situations—horses win "by noses" all the time and take home significantly more money and glory than their finish-line companions.

I am sure you have deduced the relevance of such examples to the practice of law and to the Successful Lawyer program. Many good lawyers think that the extraordinary achievers, the lawyers with exemplary practices to whom we all look up, are twice as good or three times as good as the rest of us will ever be, or ever can be. That is nonsense. The very best in the profession are only slightly better than the other good members of the profession.

Keep in mind as you work your way through this book that those who have phenomenal success financially in attracting the kind of clientele they want to serve are *not* twice as good at attaining this kind of success as others are: they are only slightly better than everybody else. Winners consistently surpass the performance of their peers because they *continually improve* in *small incremental* steps. That is the secret to their success.

I promise you that if you

1) work through this program sequentially, with your journal open and close at hand,
2) accept only those ideas and suggestions you think will have value to you,
3) create only those actions you think will be highly rewarding and have a high yield for you, and
4) implement those ideas in small incremental steps,

by the time you conclude this program you will be on your way to a much healthier and much more satisfying practice.

Ready to Move Forward

Think of this program as a journey—a journey from where you are standing now to a future you would prefer; a journey to the kind of practice that will offer you more exciting work, more challenging work,

work that you enjoy more. Work that is more fun. Work that you do for people you enjoy, for clients who are going somewhere.

The methodologies contained in this program are practical, and everyone who reads this book can implement them. In addition to strategies and guidance, however, this program offers readers an opportunity to gain a much greater confidence in their ability to control their destiny.

And so, let us begin.

Designed for Use

This book covers many subjects and it is recommended that you proceed through them sequentially. They have been carefully set out so that one idea builds on another for maximum reader benefit and understanding. However, if there are particular subjects that are of a timely nature and are therefore of particular interest to you now, use the Index and/or the Table of Contents and jump to them as you see fit. The book is constructed to allow you informed access to the parts you need when you need them, even as you progress through the material in the recommended order.

The program outlined in this book is also well supported on an immediate, real-time basis. Our Web site address is **www.successfullawyer.com**, and we invite you to gather further information there. You are also welcome to e-mail me at Edge International directly—I'm at *riskin@edge.ai*.

Part I

The Foundations of Success

Chapter 1

Imaginative Planning

Effective planning can make the difference between achieving your goals in life and not achieving them. This statement may seem self evident, but just because it is true does not mean that most people get around to putting it into practice. In working toward any kind of personal or professional success, planning is one of the most important subjects you can consider.

I am not referring to the kind of planning many large firms do when they create a 72-page report that no one reads and that does nothing but gather dust. I am talking about a personal, living plan that is customized for you.

This plan is going to take you where you want to go. It is going to take you to the kind of practice, the kind of clients, and the kind of financial and personal rewards that *you* seek to achieve.

Activating the Right Mind-Set

Before you get into creating a plan for your future, it is necessary to consciously dispense with the kind of "small-c conservative" mind-set that we as lawyers require on a daily basis in our practices. Lawyers are paid to prevent problems by foreseeing them and avoiding them, and that makes us careful. From the time we decided to go to law school, we have been cautious, choosing our educational paths and then achieving grades and scholarships with a view to being accepted by the firms that appealed to us. This necessary caution, combined with our highly analytical natures, means that lawyers naturally tend to think about any plan or course of action in terms of its consequences in the real world, and then to come to a conservative conclusion.

If you apply the same conservative approach to planning the kind of future you would like to have, that future is going to be limited and lackluster. For example, if I asked a typically conservative, cautious lawyer if he or she would like to be the world's best environmental lawyer, he or she might respond, "Oh, no! Well, I mean that would be impossible. Can you imagine? There are already mega-firms with huge practice groups. . . . There are very sophisticated legal minds. . . ." You get my drift.

The fact is that we frequently destroy our dreams before we even allow ourselves to formulate them. In order for your planning to be successful, you must paint a picture in your own mind of the kind of perfect practice you would like to have. This requires courage. It requires you to dispense with long-standing attitudes. It means that you need to throw caution to the wind. It is a necessary step.

Here is an example. Right now, use your hand to cover the next paragraphs, and then answer the following question honestly before you raise your hand again and read on:

"How much income would you like to earn as a lawyer?"

Got the answer? Write it down. Okay. Now, continue reading—

Most lawyers answer that question by suggesting that they would like to be paid at a level commensurate with other good-quality lawyers in their community.

Isn't that a nice answer?

Isn't that a safe answer?

As we all know, lawyers can achieve enormous incomes in their practices. You may have read about one particular law firm that was involved in a tobacco case on a contingency basis. Their fee was in the hundreds of millions. There are only seventy lawyers in that firm, and their recent problem has been to figure out how to distribute $300 million a year for the next thirty years.

I am not suggesting that you dream of a practice that produces mega-millions for you every month. What I am suggesting is that you *allow yourself* to paint a mental picture of what you would *like* to have. What kind of practice do you want? What kind of income? What kind of clients?

The Foundation of Your Plan

Think of a matter or case that you worked on in the last two years or so that you found particularly rewarding. Do not read on until you have selected a case or matter for consideration here, or you might as well toss this book in the fireplace.

Okay. Two attributes of this matter are extremely important to your future—its nature (the kind of matter it was), and what you brought to it. In your notebook, write a brief description of it. Explain what type of case it was—a merger or an acquisition, for example. Maybe it was a defense in a criminal matter. Perhaps it was a bid to save a park in the middle of the city. This gives you an insight into your area of passion for the practice.

Now think about what you brought to the case or matter that was special. What did you offer the client or contribute to the outcome that was unique? What did you do that was different from what the client would have experienced with some other firm, or by picking a lawyer at random? Do not be modest here. This is just you and your notebook: you don't need to be humble. Write down what you did that was special.

In this exercise, some lawyers report that what they contributed to their memorable case was synergistic—they drew a number of different disciplines together in a meaningful way, and when various areas of expertise were brought to bear on the problem, a solution emerged that might not otherwise have been found. Other lawyers report successes of an altruistic nature: perhaps they helped to save a unique ecological area—perhaps they got no fees for it, but they liked the way the outcome made them feel. Others were proud of the amount they obtained. "It was such a huge deal," they say, "it was satisfying just because of the millions involved. It didn't matter whether the fee was all that big or not, it was just the amount that made it significant for me." For still others it was indeed the fee they were able to command that meant so much to them in retrospect, because of the financial benefit to the practice or the firm.

Reflect again about the matter that you wrote down in your notebook. Ensure that you have honestly described what was, for you, the unique nature of the matter, and what unique skills you applied to it that made it so satisfying for you.

Now combine the two attributes to gain insight into what you truly like and want to do. If helping the underdog is a much bigger thrill than doing a big plain-vanilla deal, then maybe you will want a practice where the Robin Hood cases are a more significant part of the mix. If you like to organize synergistic solutions, then maybe you will want to work on matters involving different disciplines—some forms of specialized litigation, perhaps intellectual property.

If you look at them carefully, these statements will reveal to you what you enjoy most about the practice of law—the nature of the matters you like, the nature of the matters you want.

Envisioning Your Future

All right now. Based on the type of legal work you want and like, and assuming that you want to make a good living—that goes without saying—imagine for a moment that your fairy godmother has just walked into your office. She says "Look, I'm busy. I have other lawyers to see. You have about twenty seconds. Now, what kind of practice do you want?"

What do you tell her?

Think about that. Take a moment and write down your answer.

Now you have the beginning of a plan.

A Planning Exercise

Over the years we at Edge International have developed a number of tools to help individuals learn to plan effectively. Our feedback from the particular planning exercise that I am about to describe to you has shown that the practitioners who have used it have found it to be highly effective for them.

Again, you will need your notebook. It is very important to the success of this exercise that you record your responses in each section.

PART A

Imagine that it is two years from now—whatever the date is today, it is exactly two years hence. You have been away from your practice, writing a textbook in an area of law that is important to you, teaching at a prestigious school, sailing around the world, whatever. Now, after two years, you return to your practice—and it is phenomenal! Your fairy godmother has come through. As if by magic, in your absence your practice has become exactly as you dreamed it.

Now, I am going to give you the beginnings of some statements about that practice and I want you to complete them—seriously, but with your "small-c conservative" cap stowed in your attaché case. Take time to actually write down your answers.

Statement 1: My clients view me as _____.
(Finish that sentence: that is, describe how your clients view you in the perfect world that you are picturing two years from now.)

Statement 2: Other professionals see me as _____.

Statement 3: My support staff (or, if you are a partner and you have associates working with you, My support staff and associates) are feeling _____. (In this perfect world, how do these people feel about *their* work?)

Statement 4: The values and behavior that I reward are _____. (In this perfect practice, what values and behaviors in yourself and in others do you find worthy of reward? Note that "reward" here does not necessarily relate directly to the compensation system, which you may or may not control or even influence very much. "Reward" here includes positive reinforcement and recognition, and/or perhaps represents the kind of behavior that you feel commands respect.)

PART B

When contemplating change, it is important to identify aspects you *do not* want to alter. To help you do that, answer the following question:

Now that you are in this perfect world, what single aspect or aspects of your practice that you were proudest of two years ago (i.e., "today") are you glad is/are unchanged?

Write it (or them) down.

PART C

What areas of concern in your practice two years ago (i.e., "today") are you glad have been resolved?

(This gives you an opportunity to write down what is not right about your practice now. Be very specific and thorough here.)

PART D

The next step is to revise the first four statements from Part A so that they reflect your current situation. For example, in the first statement, given the reality of your practice as it exists at this moment, how do your clients view you?

Statement 1: Today, my clients view me as _____.

Statement 2: Today, other professionals see me as _____.

Statement 3: Today, my support staff (or My support staff and associates) are feeling _____ about their work.

Statement 4: The values and behaviors that I reward today are _____.

PART E

The magic of this exercise has nothing to do with fairy godmothers. The magic is in comparing the two pictures. Take a look at the kind of practice you would describe in a perfect world two years from now, and take a look at the practice you have described today. Are the pictures different?

What you need to do now is to draft a *statement of objective* for every area of dissonance between the picture of your perfect practice two years hence and your practice today.

Developing Statements of Objective

The objectives that firms develop in the work I do with them include statements such as the following: "to enhance the quality of our practice and make the quality more consistent," "to enhance the perception of clients of the quality of our practice," "to enhance our skills in [some particular area]," " to more effectively transfer skills to juniors," and so on. In your personal plan, for these statements to be effective they need to be personalized to *you*. They must emerge from *your* assessment of the present and *your* picture of the future.

Let us say that in your perfect world your clients would see you as a top expert in the field of environmental law. Today your clients view you as a quality lawyer but not necessarily a specialist. In this case, the statement of objective you would draft would be, "My objective is to become perceived as an expert in environmental law."

At this point in the process, you will have drafted several statements of objective. These give an overview as to the kinds of changes you would like to achieve.

Chapter 2

Brainstorming to Implementation

The next step in your planning process is to engage in brainstorming.

Many of us have been introduced to the art of brainstorming at some point in our lives, but as lawyers if we ever had any skills in the area, we have since had them nearly surgically removed. Consider Brainstorming Rule Number One: "Say everything that comes to mind." This is completely inconsistent with our training. We have been taught, "Think before you speak." Now I am telling you to "Speak before you think." However, as you follow your quest to steer your practice in more stimulating and rewarding directions, it is necessary to learn to distinguish between times when you need and want to be critical and analytical, and times when you need and want to be creative.

You are about to start building on the imaginative planning of the previous chapter to create a list of alternative actions to help you meet your goals. You are creating a menu of options available to you that will help you to achieve the kinds of changes you would like to achieve. You want to create the most comprehensive, most diverse, most innovative list you possibly can, and a brainstorming approach is one of the best ways you can do that. Why? Because you want to create a great menu of action options from which to choose, including unique and imaginative ones. Later, when choosing the actual actions you will implement, you will have an opportunity to be selective and discerning. Now is the time for untrammelled creativity.

The Preliminaries

Before you begin your brainstorming session, review the following rules:

Rule 1: Write down everything that comes to mind.

Rule 2: No crossing out of ideas at this stage. (As lawyers, we tend to reflect on and review everything, probably because in groups we are so critical and analytical that we feel we have to protect an idea from the assault that is likely to attack it the minute we have said it. In a brainstorming session, however, our goal is to develop a list of alternatives as quickly as we possibly can. We will analyze them later.)

Rule 3: No value judgments. Value judgments are a little easier to control if you are on your own than if you are in a group, but you still need to be wary of them—both positive and negative value judgments. During the brainstorming session, try to avoid even thinking "Hey, good idea!" or "That's a terrible idea! I know a firm that did that, and they are out of business." If you do not follow this rule, your creativity will dry up in short order.

Rule 4: Piggybacking on other ideas is encouraged. Suppose in a moment of creativity you come up with something "off the wall," like "I will hire an airplane to drop my business cards over a football field during a big game." Admittedly, this is a bit bizarre, but if you ponder the intent of this idea for a moment, you might think: "Okay, so what are some other options for getting blanket coverage in a particular community? How about taking out an ad in the football program congratulating the team on getting to the finals?" The point is that great ideas often emerge from crazy or unusable ones, and if we are too rigid in our thinking, we may simply not allow for diversity at all. Aside from being less useful, mundane ideas create less competitive advantage—and they are simply not as much fun to execute. So remember that apparently stupid or ridiculous ideas can often lead to far more brilliant ones, and let one idea lead to another: that is the nature of the brainstorming activity.

List Actions, Not Ideas

When we talk about "taking action," we move into another area of vulnerability for many lawyers. As I mentioned previously, studies show that lawyers grasp concepts faster than any other identifiable group in society. This is basically good news, because it means that we are able to identify issues quickly. However, the ability to grasp concepts can lead us to think conceptually so often that "concepts" and "actions" become confused. As you are brainstorming, you will need to be extremely specific, and to make certain at each step that you are putting *actions* rather than concepts or ideas on the list or menu you are creating.

Here is an example. If you are brainstorming around the goal of enhancing client-satisfaction levels, you might write, "Communicate more with key clients." This *is* a good idea, but it is not an action.

I have devised a test that you can use to determine whether something is an action or not. I call it the "telephone delegation test." If you can pick up a telephone and delegate it, it is an action. If you cannot, it is a concept. For example, let us imagine that after the brainstorming session, you say to your secretary, "I have decided to communicate a little better with my key clients. Will you get on that for me please?" The secretary is likely to reply, "Could you be a bit more specific about what you want me to do?"

How you respond to that request gets you closer to the difference between actions and concepts. If your goal is to communicate better with key clients, how do you do that? How do you begin? Well, perhaps first you will need to identify who you consider your "key clients" to be. Maybe you will ask your secretary to print up a client list that you can go through with coloured markers. In this case, the action you write down will be, "Identify key clients by color-coding list."

Next you will need to decide how you will communicate. What are your options? Well, you can visit key clients. You can write to key clients. You can telephone key clients. Now you are developing a list of optional *actions* that can actually be implemented. And that is the goal of this exercise.

The Brainstorming Session

For each of the statements of objective that you created in Chapter 1 to describe a change you want to achieve in your practice, brainstorm a list of specific alternative actions that you could take—actions that might help you move from where you are to that perfect picture you described two years hence. Write them down in your journal. Your goal is to find at least three to five actions, ranging from the ridiculous to the sublime, for each statement of objective. Remember to

- write down every action you can think of, without value judgment or discussion;
- allow yourself to piggyback on your own ideas;
- list actions, not concepts.

Think divergently. Let yourself go. Have fun.

Following Up

Some people are nervous about the brainstorming process. They say, "Just a moment. You've told me to speak (or write) before I think. You've told me to be innovative and creative. You've said it doesn't matter how silly or ridiculous my ideas are, they still have to go down on paper. What's to prevent my ending up with a silly, preposterous action plan?"

After you have created this innovative list of actions for each statement of objective, you do not have a plan of action—yet. What you have now is a menu, or series of menus. It is at this point that you are allowed to be critical and analytical. This is the time for you to be discerning. This is the time when you are able to put your wisdom to the test.

This is also the time to be realistic.

Sometimes when I am working with groups or firms, highly worthwhile actions will be identified, but then later when we go around the room and ask who feels so strongly about these actions that they would actually be prepared to roll up their sleeves and contribute to them, no one volunteers. At times like that, I take a marker pen and draw a line very carefully through the action under discussion. I usually hear gasps: "You can't take that off the list. That's skillbuilding! We've got to do that." My question in such circumstances is, "Why deceive yourselves? If no one in the room feels strongly enough about it or enthusiastic enough about it to actually roll up their sleeves and contribute to it, then why keep it on the list? It is not going to get done anyway."

A discussion or debate usually ensues, and that is when we really decide whether the action is important. If it is, we decide what piece or part of it really needs to be done.

Think about this in terms of your own planning. When you created your list of possible actions, you were applying your creativity. You were brainstorming all kinds of possibilities. Now these options must meet reality. Now is the time to assess whether you actually feel these actions are important enough that you are prepared to allocate real time to them.

Be very discerning about which actions you choose from the list. Choose only those things you feel most strongly about. Choose very few, and ensure that the ones you choose pass two tests. Ask yourself:

1. Will implementing this action have a high yield for me? Will it be highly effective? Will I get a good rate of return?
2. Do I feel strongly enough about this action that I am likely to apply the discipline I need to really get it done?

There will be many actions on the list that you will think you should be doing, and perhaps you should. But you will not. You will do one or two, so choose only one or two. Remember that doing even one will give you a tremendous competitive advantage.

Those who take one action or maybe two from their lists and really put them into practice are miles ahead of those who take many actions but wind up doing none. Use your journal to help you with the discipline of actually doing this. This will also give you a convenient place to review your thoughts and, if necessary, revise them in the future.

Chapter 3

The Mount Everest Syndrome

In many firms, good lawyers with good minds who are contemplating desirable changes, perhaps to address specific problems, will decide on overly grandiose initiatives that they can never actually achieve. Perhaps, for example, in response to a comment by someone that people in the office are out of shape and look rather sleepy by 5 P.M., somebody will say, "Maybe we should go for some hikes around here—get the blood pumping, get ourselves into better shape. That might make us better lawyers and make us happier."

Typically, within about a nanosecond somebody else in the group will say, "Look, if we're going to do some hiking, given the nature of our firm, we really ought to be climbing Everest. I mean, what kind of firm are we? We don't want to be second-tier. If we are going to take on a project like this, we're going to do it at the top of the curve."

Now the group needs a volunteer. Perhaps one of them has seen a documentary about climbing Everest—knows what a Sherpa is, knows what oxygen tanks look like, knows that you need tents at a base camp, that maybe you should have a helicopter, and so on. So that person volunteers to look into climbing Mount Everest. (Needless to say, in the case of a sole practitioner, these three speakers—the originator of the idea, the elaborator of the idea, and the volunteer—are all the same person.) A month later when the group gets together (or when the sole practitioner reviews his or her plans), the answer to "What has been accomplished in regard to the Everest climb?" is—nothing.

The fact that nothing has happened on the Everest initiative is far less important at this point than what happens next.

In group settings in this type of situation, two questions are typically asked by those present. (They are usually asked silently: the partners already know the answers.) The first question is this: "What are this individual's billings like? Are they pretty good? Yes? Good. Okay, then, we're almost there." Second question: "Does this individual attract a fair amount of business? Bit of a rainmaker? Yes? Okay, we're there. We're not going to trouble this individual over some nutty idea to climb Everest. After all, the mountain will wait. We can always do it next year." In essence, what that group has done is to forgive that individual. Similarly, sole practitioners or lawyers working on individual projects will look for justifications in order to forgive themselves.

But look at the syndrome that has developed: Promise big, deliver nothing, be forgiven. Promise big, deliver nothing, be forgiven. Whether this scenario is occurring in a mega-firm meeting, in a small group, or on an individual basis, the need to forgive and move on month after month is a losing syndrome. Champions do not do this.

Two simple steps will allow you to avoid becoming involved in the Mount Everest Syndrome ever again. These steps are useful both in your leadership of others and in your guidance of yourself.

Achievable Actions

In the previous chapter we carefully examined the difference between a concept and an action. Your first step in avoiding the Mount Everest Syndrome is to be very certain that you are indeed creating specific actions rather than concepts—actions with potentially positive outcomes that are viable in your practice. The second step, which is also critically important, is that you take on, in a logical sequence, only bite-sized pieces of those actions. So in managing our friend who was looking into climbing Everest for example, you could ask that individual, "What is your first step? What are you going to do first? What will happen over the next few days?"

To provide a more realistic example from a professional practice point of view, imagine that you have decided that you want to write an article. Perhaps it relates to a matter you are dealing with in your practice—you are going to tie together intellectual property aspects with employment law, let us say, and you feel that by creating an article on that subject you will impress some appropriate clients or prospective clients. This is a great idea.

What typically happens at this juncture is that you say to yourself, "Well, how long will it take to get that article done? Four weeks, six weeks?"

"Six weeks," you may answer, giving yourself plenty of time.

Six weeks later, what has happened? Nothing.

So what do you do now? Shoot yourself? Feel guilty? Feel like you are unable to accomplish anything? Feel your self-esteem diminished? Feel like this is all a waste of time? After that, do you forgive yourself?

To avoid the Mount Everest Syndrome, you must break your task down into small components. Because as lawyers we tend to be cerebral and to think conceptually, very frequently we do not pause to break the task down into its component parts, thus allowing ourselves to move forward incrementally. If you describe three or four or five or six phases to getting the article done, you *will* be able to move forward.

Whether you are managing yourself or managing others, the critical first questions for any task are these:

- What needs to be done first?
- What must happen over the next few days?

In the case of the article, the first step may be to identify subjects for the article, and here I mean *specific* subjects—i.e., a general outline of the contents. Getting a list of the specific subject matter for the article done within three or four days is a definite move in the right direction. You are moving from concept to action. No longer are you spinning your wheels: you now have traction. Ultimately, even if it takes eight weeks to write the article rather than the six you first projected, you *will* get the thing done. In fact, it will probably take you less time than you had thought.

People who kid themselves, who have grandiose plans and never get started, are the ones who soon decide that it is worthless and futile to make plans in the first place. They give up completely. I assure you that if you plan in the manner I have described, and if you set for yourself *realistic* actions and break them down into *incremental* portions and follow them *one step after the other*, you will leave your competition in the dust. Why? Because your competitors suffer from the Mount Everest Syndrome, too.

Return to your journal and look at the action items you created in the last chapter. Break them down into incremental steps and track your progress. The lesson in this chapter is powerful only when applied.

Getting to Base Camp

There is another enemy that can stand between us and the accomplishment of our objectives, and if you are not careful it will stand between you and the achievement of the actions you set for yourself during the planning process. This is the problem: at any particular moment, if there is a competition between an action you have selected and some billable work for a client, you will likely default to the billable work. Now, that is the right decision 99 percent of the time. However, it is not the right decision 100 percent of the time. You must allocate time to complete your action plan or you will never achieve your goals.

Look at your working schedule. Month by month, are you budgeting any time at all to get your actions accomplished? It doesn't really matter what amount of time you decide to budget—an hour a week or an hour a day—but it *is* necessary to set aside some specific amount of time that you think is appropriate for you, given your lifestyle and the pressures of your practice. Then you must treat that nonbillable time as sacred. If you fail to do that, you will never accomplish the actions you have set out for yourself.

What I have seen from superb practitioners or, in other words, what I have observed of best practices, is that the winners are the ones who do allocate or assign a portion of their time to accomplishing their predetermined actions. It may be a small amount of time but they assign some. On the time sheets of one enormously successful firm, one hour of every day must be devoted to work on some of the actions that the firm has set, individual by individual, and must be accounted for in that way. There is a slogan in that firm that says, "One hour of nonbillable time is worth more than an hour of billable time." Now, they do not mean that at the end of the day if you have spent ten nonbillable hours and zero billable hours you are an asset to the organization. What they mean is, if you have failed to spend at least one quality, nonbillable hour in the day then you have failed to achieve something far more important than the billable time you have achieved.

Will it be an hour a day or an hour a week? You must be the judge of that, but whatever you decide, budget it, allocate it, put it in your planner—do that now, if possible—and then use that time in the way it is intended, toward the accomplishment of your actions. When you look back over a period of weeks and months, you will begin to see a change, an incremental rate of progress, and that progress will begin to separate you from your competitors.

Chapter 4

Specialty Versus Commodity Work

Almost everyone enjoys an occasional Pepsi or Coca-Cola (or Diet Pepsi or Diet Coca-Cola). Every time you enjoy such a beverage you expect it to taste somewhat the way it tasted the last time, and usually it does. When you pour one of those beverages into a glass you do not expect to see animal parts or other strange objects floating around in it (if you did, you likely would not be interested in acquiring more of the product very soon). In addition, if you look at the packaging, you will see that it is highly consistent too, usually unflawed.

When I am working with a firm of professionals, I present this idea of "the tangible product," and then I ask the group, "What is your product? What do you sell? Can you show me one? Did you bring any with you?"

Most professionals instinctively know that what they provide to their clientele is something very different than tangible items. All the rules for selling a Midas muffler or pots and pans simply seem irrelevant to a profession. That is because, of course, the interface between a professional and a client is not a product at all. It is something far less tangible. Therefore, typical responses to my questions are, "Well, I think we sell a service," or "I think we sell our knowledge."

The answers vary but the bottom line is that after reflection, most professionals realize that what we sell is ourselves. Our knowledge and skill is part of that. Certainly these are sometimes packaged into document form or report form, but basically we sell knowledge and expertise.

The Nature of Our Service

It is important to reflect upon the spectrum of services we provide, and to distinguish those which are considered "specialties" from those which are considered "commodities." This assessment will provide insights into what clients will expect and/or tolerate from the professional who provides the service.

By way of an example of a specialist, there is a litigator in Washington, D.C., who is also a chemist—a brilliant scientist, in fact. If something happens in a laboratory of a big oil company that might endanger workers, this man is called in. He knows how to construct tests and, if possible (i.e., where appropriate and supported by the truth) to make findings that exonerate the owners of the laboratory. His value is, obviously, tremendous. His hourly rate is astronomical. This man offers a *specialty* service.

Now think for a moment about a lawyer who does routine mortgage work or routine residential real-estate transactions. We know that when you acquire a house you are as likely to get an equally good title from one real-estate lawyer as another. Certainly problems arise from time to time, and certainly in more specialized situations there may be environmental issues or other concerns that require a specialist, but for the typical residential transaction, there aren't too many specialized issues. That kind of work might therefore be considered a *commodity*.

Despite the fact that we are not selling products, a couple of specialty versus commodity examples from the retail world are pertinent to this subject. First, imagine for a moment that the head of state for your country wants to visit your firm as part of a public-relations initiative. You will get national press coverage, and in exchange all you need to do is provide some hors d'oeuvres for the head of state and his or her entourage.

Now a catering broker comes by and tells you that he knows some students at a local university who are starting a catering business, and that he can get you a price from them that is about 25 percent below the market rate. He also knows some specialists in the catering business who have dealt with heads of state before. They are probably 25 percent over market, but they can handle your needs quite nicely. Without blinking, most professionals will choose to pay above-market prices for highly experienced professional caterers who have dealt with heads of state before. These caterers can be considered "specialists."

Now let us look at a situation relating to commodities. Your spouse asks you to come home with a case of Coca-Cola. You hear that a gas station on your way home from work is giving away cases of Coca-Cola today to anyone who fills up their tank *and* that their fuel prices are competitive *and* that it does not matter how much fuel you need; as long as you fill up, they will give you a free case. What do you do? Get the case free from the gas station, or buy it at premium rates from your local convenience store?

Most people to whom I put that question quickly decide that—unless there is some specific reason for patronizing the local convenience store or avoiding the gas station—they would take the free case and get their car refueled. Why? Because they know that there is no appreciable difference between what they will pay for at the convenience store and what they will get free today at the gas station. A case of Coca-Cola is something that we see as being the same no matter where we get it. As I said earlier, Coca-Cola manufacturers spend a lot of money to make sure that the quality is consistent, to make sure that the labeling is always pristine—and they do that so we can rely upon and trust the product. It is a commodity.

Where does this leave you? The commodity services you provide, like Coca-Cola, are going to be greeted with fee resistance. However, in the specialty areas of your practice, you will see less fee resistance—especially if you are able to convey convincingly the specialty attributes of the service (for specific information on doing this, see Chapter 45, "Overcoming Fee Resistance").

The Importance of the Client Relationship

I have taken you on an in-depth examination of the distinction between a commodity and a specialty because I believe that your awareness of the difference between the two—and your determination as a professional as to which (if any) of the services you provide are commodities, and which (if any) are specialties—is fundamental to the manner in which you present yourself, build relationships, and market yourself.

You may want to note in your journal the categories of work you do and their basic subcomponents and be brutally honest with yourself in labeling them as "specialty" or "commodity." If you are in doubt on an item, it's probably "commodity."

Those who are providing specialty services need to concentrate on the substantive nature of what they do. Clients and prospective clients are far less sensitive about the "bedside manner" and other service attributes of specialists than they are in situations where commodities are provided. However, the majority of the work that lawyers do has more in common with "commodities" than "specialties." And clearly, as professionals, we are not in a position where better packaging, more consistent packaging, and other simple quality issues can assure us of successful futures. The interface between ourselves and our clients is not a product: it is us. We are in a profession that has a great deal to do with the relationship between our clients and ourselves.

Many lawyers cling to the myth that hard work and dedication alone entitle them to high levels of appreciation from existing clients, and ensure their selection by prospective clients. This view is naive to the point of being dangerous to the financial health of their firms. Traditional high-quality intellect- and knowledge-based lawyering skills are necessary but not sufficient for a prosperous practice today. As one professional put it, "Most clients want to know how much you care before they care how much you know." Lawyers need to think about how their clients *feel* as much as they do about what they *need*.

You may not want to hear that. Most of our training as professionals has been technical. We have been taught to identify legal issues. We have been taught to see legal problems. We have been taught to prevent problems or provide solutions arising from the law. Sometimes it does not occur to us that the client wants far more than a solution.

Your client wants to know whether you understand the problem. Your client wants to know whether you understand how he or she *feels* about the problem. Your client wants to know whether you understand how *badly* he or she wants a solution to the problem.

Particularly in the case of commodity work—although it certainly doesn't hurt in the case of specialty work as well—the successful professional learns how to empathize with the client. The successful professional not only understands the client's perspective, but also *lets the client know* that he or she understands.

The next section of this book focuses on the lawyer-client relationship.

Part II

Successfully Managing the Client Relationship

Chapter 5

Introduction to Client-Relations Skills

I began my law career in the 1970s in a hundred-year-old Canadian firm with some of the best lawyers in practice either then or today. They believed that if you had a good education, you went to a good firm, and you did high-quality work for good clients, your practice would be successful. And they were right—at the time.

That prescription for a successful law practice is no longer useful. In the intervening years, a range of factors have had significant impact on the practice of law, including competitive threats from other professions, the high degree of specialization of lawyers, the advent and application of technology, and the fact that knowledge is depreciating much faster than ever before. Today it is necessary for good professionals not only to deliver excellence, but to be able to convey their value to clients and prospective clients.

In the next chapters you are going to be introduced to specific client-relations skills. The skills that we are going to review range from what some call the "soft" underlying skills, like listening or managing expectations, to more-aggressive results-oriented skills, such as courting and meeting prospective clients.

A Public-Relations Spectrum

In the past number of years I have had the opportunity to serve a wide variety of professional-service firms, both large and small, in many countries and in different cultures. At least one attribute is common to them all: they know how to deal effectively with clients.

The distribution of this ability within the firm might be visualized in the form of a bell curve. At the top of the curve are approximately 10 percent of the professionals who are gifted when it comes to client relations. These people are not clones of one another, by the way—in fact, their personalities and communication styles are quite diverse. At the base of the curve is another 10 percent. These people may produce great legal work, but they are certainly not your "public relations" types. Managing partners joke that "We'd like to feed them the work through the top of the door and pull it out the bottom. In a perfect world, they would never meet a client."

When it comes to client-relations skills, most lawyers fall into the 80 percent between the PR experts and the socially dysfunctional. What we want to examine in this section is how those in the middle 80 percent can acquire the skills of the gifted top 10 percent.

Client-Relations Skills Can Be Learned

There is a myth that some people are born to be great rainmakers and others are not. That is absolute nonsense. The most effective rainmakers are those who have learned some specific skills over their lifetimes which make them more effective with people. Some of them learned these skills at their parents' knees, others at school or in places they worked before they became lawyers—maybe even in the sales or marketing fields. Wherever those skills were acquired, those rainmakers we now see as the so-called naturals are those who can employ human relations skills effectively at will.

We send litigators to advocacy courses because we believe that such courses will enhance the skill levels of those advocates, thereby increasing their value. There is no difference between enhancing advocacy skills and enhancing rainmaking skills. Both sets of skills can be taught, and both sets of skills can be learned.

In the next few chapters you will be introduced to the specific skills that I have observed in the best rainmakers in the world. Learning and using these skills can help you to become more effective both in enhancing existing client-satisfaction levels, and in attracting prospective clients.

Chapter 6

Courting Prospective Clients

You will notice that "courting prospective clients" and "meeting prospective clients" are separate chapters in this book. Many lawyers consider the two steps as one. They think, "If there's a prospective client we would like to act for, and don't already act for, then we should court them and meet them, and get retained by them."

In fact, "courting" prospective clients is a step that we as lawyers tend to overlook, and we need to give it some serious consideration.

In the course of our practices and our daily lives, we meet prospective clients all the time. Think of how often you go to a meeting or a reception or some other function and exchange business cards with someone you might like to serve. Most of us take those business cards back to our offices, and we put them in a drawer. We have good intentions about following up with those people, but by the time we get around to it we feel a little awkward because so much time has passed. Then a little more time goes by and it becomes quite impossible to follow up, and finally there comes a time when we look in the drawer and we look through those cards, and we can no longer even remember who the people are who gave them to us. This is human nature.

When you are courting prospective clients, however, you need to take action very quickly with those cards, whenever it is appropriate.

When is it appropriate to take action? Well, imagine that you have just met a prospective client. Now answer the following questions: Why do you consider this individual to be a prospective client? What kind of work do you think you could be doing for this person? Can you state in a few words what special skill or experience of yours would be highly beneficial to this client?

If you feel that your skill and experience in a specific area do not exceed those of other practitioners in your community, is there some other level at which you are unique and could provide real benefit to this person? Perhaps on the service level? Or even on the value level? (In regard to value, I am not suggesting that the way to build a practice is to reduce fees until you are the cheapest game in town. That is not a winning strategy. On the other hand, if you have developed processes within your firm that allow you to produce work in some specific area extremely efficiently, you may be able to pass on that work for a fair fee that gives you a good return but is competitive to other providers.)

In other words, Step One of the courting process is to think about *What is in it for the client?* Why would it be beneficial for this person if you were to serve them? If you have not worked out the answer to that question, there is no point in picking up the phone. However, do not "cop out" on this question. Do not let your inability to answer it serve as an excuse not to pursue the prospective client. The winning practice—the best practice—at this stage is to spend a little time focusing, either by yourself or with your fellow practitioners, on what benefits you can offer, and then to follow up.

Making the Call

The heart of courting prospective clients is picking up that telephone and calling that person whose acquaintance you have made. If you have been strategic and forward-thinking, then perhaps during the reception or the luncheon or the party, or wherever you met that person, you actually began to talk about your work area, or mentioned an article you thought might be of value, or referred to some checklist or some other resource that you thought that person might find useful. In that case, you have an advantage because you can now simply follow up by telephone. If you have not laid groundwork for the call, think now about what you might provide instantly to the prospective client that might be of value to them even before you begin serving them formally.

Some professionals feel they need to develop rapport with prospective clients before they can talk business. If you are more comfortable saying, "Let's go to a game," or "Let's just go for lunch. It'd be fun to get to know you a little better," fine—as long as this is not an excuse to put off forever the possibility of talking about business.

In my experience, however, the direct approach is often the most effective. Let prospective clients know that you have something that you think might be of immediate interest, perhaps an article or a checklist or some thoughts on a specific subject. Or explain perhaps that you are interested in obtaining some information from someone in that person's industry that will help you serve your existing clients better—this is also an approach that is quite appealing to prospective clients. Most will be quite willing to meet with you to discuss such proposals further.

In achieving a first meeting, some of the best and most effective rainmakers use a simple technique that might seem to you at first a little tacky. Instead of asking prospective clients whether they would like to go for lunch, to which the answer can be a polite "yes," or a polite "no," they say instead, "Look. Why don't we get together for lunch? I've got a couple of options available to me: Tuesday is free, but if that doesn't work for you, then how about Friday?"

This technique is imported from other realms and is based on the principle that while both questions offer options, the first involves a yes-no binary choice—"Yes, I will" or "No, I won't." The most likely answers to the second question, on the other hand, are both "yes"—"Yes, lunch on Tuesday," or "Yes, lunch on Friday." If you are uncomfortable with this approach, obviously you shouldn't use it—but giving optional times is a device many effective rainmakers find useful when they are suggesting get-togethers. It makes it far more likely that the client will say "yes."

Building Your Courtship Skills

In essence, "courting clients" is about 1) knowing what you have that may be of value to a prospective client, 2) picking up the phone, and 3) arranging a meeting. Many lawyers lack the skills or the confidence to successfully court clients. You can develop your own skills and confidence in this area by considering the following questions:

- Have you determined what you can offer that is of genuine value, by way of substance or method of delivery or efficiency or some other attribute, so that you can look prospective clients straight in the eye and offer them something they will find advantageous to them?

- Can you overcome the propensity to procrastinate (e.g., to put the business card away in the drawer) in order to take action quickly?
- Are you comfortable using a simple technique that is far more likely to result in a "yes" response—and in a commitment to meet with you—than a binary choice would be?

I suggest you take action now by identifying at least one potential client you have been putting off contacting. Use your journal and note a strategy for making contact—is there an article you can send? If not, what other approach might make sense?

One of the best lawyers I have seen in the area of courting clients thinks of everybody he meets as fitting into one of two categories: they are either existing clients, or they are about to become existing clients and simply don't know it yet. That is a useful mind-set.

> Lawyers who know the kind of practice they want to have, and can clearly identify the kinds of prospective clients that can give them that practice, and have the courage to court those clients instead of just letting their business cards gather dust have a huge competitive advantage. Most people in the professions simply do not have either the skill or the courage to court clients.

Chapter 7

Meeting Prospective Clients

Sometimes the first meeting with a client is a response to a request for proposal that has been initiated by the client. More often, however, you have initiated the meeting yourself, and during the courting stage you have done the groundwork that has led up to it. This groundwork is extremely important because with it, you have begun to formulate the expectations of the prospective client for what will happen at the meeting.

As part of your planning, you should have assembled a fairly thorough analysis of the benefits to the prospective client of retaining you. You should go over these again immediately prior to your meeting.

Take Your Time

A mistake that many lawyers make when they meet with a prospective client is to hurry the conversation prematurely into a business discussion. Be patient. Whether you are meeting with a senior executive officer of a major corporation, the owner of a small business, or an individual client, most people will value your showing some interest in them personally, and will appreciate your wanting to get to know a little bit more about them. Efforts to learn more about the individual may range from admiring a trophy or a plaque in their office and asking how it was acquired, to inquiring how the individual came into the position they now hold.

Of course, you need to be sensitive to the circumstances. If you are talking to a hard-driving business tycoon, asking what is in the office aquarium could lead to a difficult moment. On the other hand, you may be dealing with a very affable individual who will be genuinely pleased if you ask about the family photos on the credenza, or about a framed portrait of a horse they have hanging on their wall.

Developing a Relationship

Once some rapport has been established, you should try to ascertain what the prospective client values from a relationship with a lawyer. Most people will have already dealt with lawyers in some capacity—or may do so routinely—and they will have some views as to what they like or what frustrates them in terms of those dealings. Finding out their feelings in this area will give you enormous evidence and ammunition to shape the kind of service you can provide, and the manner in which you will provide it. It will allow you to make the services you offer highly appealing to this particular prospective client.

The Work

Now it is time to talk about the essence of the work that you are able to provide. Many effective rainmakers suggest beginning with a step that is quite small, involving some first phase or some first service which, by itself, may seem minimal. You might say, for example, "Let me see if I can gather some facts about such-and-such for you," or, "Let me see if I can produce an outline of how a matter like this would progress," or, "Would you like me to conduct a search and see what our options are at this preliminary stage?" or something to that effect.

Successful rainmakers try to get a commitment to provide a small service for the prospective client, because they know that if they get retained to do something small, they can always grow the business later. You cannot grow work you do not have.

The essence of an effective meeting with a prospective client is communicating to the client how you can match their needs and preferences with the service you have to offer. If you are clear in your own mind about advantages that the prospective client will achieve by retaining you, you can describe those benefits to them with enthusiasm and determination. If there is a *value benefit* through efficiencies, for example, you can begin to map out a comparison between what the client is currently experiencing and what you have to offer. If you are dealing with a *skill* or a *knowledge issue*, you can provide specific examples of your achievements involving significant change to quantum or complexity that will appeal to the client and offer them confidence that you are the person to solve their problems. It is essential at this stage to convey to the prospective client, in a way that is *meaningful* to him or her, why it would be advantageous to retain you.

Use your journal to record the benefits you bring to the prospective clients you have identified. Note whether they are "value" benefits or "skill/knowledge" benefits. Note how you might communicate such benefits—or, even better, how you might demonstrate them—to the prospective client. If you have something tangible such as a testimonial from a previous client or an article about you in the press, it can be useful to share that kind of document.

Ask!

The last segment of a meeting with a prospective client involves summoning the courage to *ask* for the opportunity to do work for that individual.

For some reason, many high-quality lawyers seem to believe that if they simply talk about their expertise or knowledge or value, they will entice the client into making it easy for them by saying, "That is wonderful. Won't you please do this for me?"

Unfortunately, in the real world most of the time this does not happen. The client may have a million reasons to procrastinate.

The successful rainmaker knows how to ask to be retained at the appropriate moment—or even how to *assume* retention. For example, you might ask, "Would you like me to begin the process by looking into such-and-such?" Or you might say, "Why don't I go back and just take a look at this, and build a preliminary report for you? You can have a look at it, we can discuss fees at that time, and then we can go from there."

Here is a checklist for your first meeting with a prospective client:

1. Go into the meeting knowing the advantage for the prospective client of retaining you.
2. Be patient. Show some interest and acquire some information and knowledge about the client.
3. Find out what the prospective client wants from a relationship with a lawyer.
4. Before leaving the meeting, have the courage to implement a plan of action—either by asking for a modest amount of initial work, or even by asking to take on the entire matter.

Chapter 8

Handling Telephone Inquiries

Many of us engage in business-development activities that are designed to make the phone ring. We are pleased when we receive referrals from existing clients, or calls from people who have seen or heard about something we have done. In short, we *want* prospective clients to contact us by phone.

But what happens when a prospective client does call?

When we receive a telephone inquiry, a couple of our professional propensities often set to work against us. First of all, as lawyers we are extremely problem/solution-oriented. The minute we understand the nature of a client's problem, we feel almost compelled to advise and solve it.

The second propensity relates to discussions about our professional fees—a subject that is usually initiated by the client rather than ourselves. If a prospective client raises the subject of fees in the first phone call, most lawyers are prepared to talk about it. If we do that, however, we set ourselves up in a lose-lose situation.

If we discuss a very conservative fee, then when it comes time to bill we will find ourselves in a little box of our own creation, with no place to go. If, on the other hand, we talk about a significant fee, we are likely to frighten away the prospective client.

Take a Moment

When a first phone call from a prospective client comes in, pause and reflect upon what is in the mind of the caller. There are two things prospective clients want:

1. They want advice. They have a problem. They know you are a lawyer. They would like to put the problem in front of you and get as much counsel and help right here and now as you are prepared to give.

2. They want the very best fee arrangement possible. This is understandable; they are not in a very good position at this stage to distinguish between one fee provider and another. Why not work to secure the best terms?

Look at the vulnerability you face as the lawyer in this situation. You have a prospective client on the phone who wants free advice, who wants you to quote a fee, and who wants that quote to be the very lowest number possible.

Many lawyers are surprised to learn that they can overcome their vulnerability in this kind of potentially difficult situation, and direct it toward a very positive result. They can even use this opportunity to gain a competitive advantage over the other potential lawyers that the prospective client may call.

Secure a Meeting

Your first priority of course will be to ascertain the name of the person who is calling, and find out by whom they were referred or otherwise came to call you. This is extremely useful business-development information to have. Then, as quickly as possible, you will want to get as much information as you need in order to reasonably assess the nature of the matter about which they have called.

At this stage, the prospective client will encourage you to provide them with free advice. You need to gently resist doing this. Your job is now to persuade that person to take a little of their time to actually meet with you.

What you need to do is to suggest the potential advantages to this prospective client in getting together with you for a face-to-face meeting. Here are two basic benefits that you can point out; you may think of others:

1. A meeting will provide you with a better opportunity to determine whether you have the expertise and knowledge that will be of assistance to the prospective client; and

2. A meeting will allow the prospective client to get to know you a little better, which will put them in a better position to assess whether you are the provider they would like to choose.

Once a meeting occurs you will be at a significant advantage. When they see you face-to-face—see your expertise, see your knowledge, see your care and understanding—the prospective client's question will no longer be, "Are you the least expensive?" Instead it will become, "Will I get value for my fee?"

It is much easier for us as lawyers to answer questions about fees as they relate to value than it is to discuss whether or not we are the least expensive. Even if you are not the least expensive, by the time the prospective client has met you and begun to trust you a little bit, the lowest cost will no longer be the most important issue.

Build on Meetings

Your business-development efforts, the good relationships you have with existing clients, and other referral sources will produce a finite number of telephone inquiries for you. Your job is to maximize the number of those that you convert to client relationships.

- Remember that the prospective client has you in a vulnerable position during an initial phone call.
- Remember that the motives of the prospective client are to acquire advice and secure the best fee arrangement possible.
- Gently persuade the prospective client of the merits of meeting with you in person, thereby giving yourself an opportunity to demonstrate what you can do for them, and giving them an opportunity to determine whether they are comfortable with you.

Keep in mind that those lawyers who know how to convert a telephone inquiry into an initial consultation will build their practices much more quickly than those who do not.

Chapter 9

Active Listening

When I talk to professional firms about developing their client relations skills and we go through the list of skills they could acquire or refine, most of them do not consider the skill of listening to be very sexy, attractive, or even interesting. And yet, ironically, the most powerful, capable rainmakers in significant firms who have been through skills-training programs have told me that listening was the most important skill they acquired—by a long shot.

Now, listening does seem like one of those easy skills that is simply intuitive. Not so. In most cases, when people are listening to other people speak, they are also thinking about what they are going to say next. Listening well can be very, very challenging.

Active, effective listening involves not only concentrating and focusing on what the other person is saying, but also empathizing with how the other person feels, and then letting them know that you know how they feel.

Think about your reaction when you are trying to communicate with someone who is clearly not listening to you. What are the indicators that that other person is not listening? They may be looking at their watch, looking away from you, or in some other way failing to have eye contact with you. Even if they are looking at you, sometimes you can see from their expression that they are only thinking about what they want to say next—and when they can interrupt you to say it.

Have you ever waited to see a physician who, when he or she finally appeared, took your file or the clipboard and—while you were explaining your problem—glanced over the information that the nurse had collected, then sputtered a few words and told you about some medication he or she thought you should take? After which, either ceremoniously or unceremoniously, he or she may have waltzed off to see the next patient in the next cubicle—who had, no doubt, like you, been waiting forty-five minutes or so for their turn.

How did you feel? Did you feel as though that physician really heard or cared about you? Did it cross your mind that perhaps he or she was trying to maximize his or her income by getting as many people through those cubicles that day as possible?

Studies measuring how people perceive lawyers suggest that, as a group, we are considered to be aloof, arrogant, users of jargon, expensive, conceited, and so on. (No doubt you can add to this list.) If that is true, then we have a lot to overcome. If we are going to build the trust and confidence of our clients, we must not only overcome the bias and the bigotry against lawyers in general, we must instil into our clients the confidence that we as individual lawyers really *do* care about them. A strong step in this direction is to make sure that your clients or prospective clients know absolutely that you are concentrating when they are speaking to you. You want to *assure* them that you are listening.

Visible Listening

How do you assure someone that you are listening? Well, first of all, you need to show them that you are listening. One foolproof way is to take notes. Taking notes is a highly visible sign that you are concentrating and tracking what the client is saying. (Obviously, notes will also help you later, when you are reflecting upon the interview.)

It is true that during a particularly sensitive interview, where the content is perhaps quite difficult or challenging, some clients may not wish to have their words recorded. As always it is necessary to use your judgment, and of course, when appropriate you will need to ask clients if they mind your taking notes. However, as a general rule, do take notes in interviews.

You must also convey to the client that you have heard what they are *feeling*. To do this, you need first to mentally identify what, in fact, their feelings are. Are they angry? Are they frustrated? Are they disappointed? Are they neutral? Are they apathetic? You need to measure their feelings, and you need to comment on the emotions you perceive.

You may say something to the client such as, "I can see this makes you very angry. I can't blame you. If someone had done this to me, I would be angry too"—or something along those lines.

Look for confirmation from the client that you are correct in your assessment. Believe me, if you are not, the client will correct you. They will say, "No, I'm not angry, it's just that . . . [this or this or that]."

In addition to reflecting the emotion back, you must also, of course, let the client know that you understand the facts. Indeed, it is a good practice to reflect back the basic facts aloud, because then if you do have them wrong the client will have a chance to correct you here as well. They will also be very reassured, again, to know that you were listening, you were tracking with them, and that you understand what the problem is.

Provide Assurance

The final step in listening is to assure the client. Assure the client that you understand how they feel. Assure the client that you understand how badly they want a result. Assure the client that you have the confidence in your own knowledge and experience that will enable you to help them solve the problem as well as anyone in the profession. Finally, assure them of your best efforts—that you will commit to giving your all, to doing whatever you can to help them.

As lawyers, we are used to responding or acknowledging the content or the facts of what our clients tell us. Everybody can do that. To gain a competitive advantage, you need to be able to demonstrate to the client that you heard the emotion as well.

If you

1) track what you are hearing, and
2) reassure the client that you understand the issue and the emotions they are feeling, and
3) reassure the client that you will use all of your abilities to help them achieve a positive result,

you will establish a connection that will far surpass the typical lawyer-client relationship.

Think back to a recent meeting you had with a client. Record in your journal what the client communicated both factually and emotionally. Record what you might have said, if you had that meeting to do over again, that would have better demonstrated your profound understanding of the facts and the emotions involved and conveyed your assurance that you could really help.

Chapter 10

Managing Client Expectations

All of us constantly measure and assess everything we encounter. Right now you are measuring and assessing the quality of this book. It is something we do every time we have a meal in a restaurant, every time we stay in a hotel, every time we hear a performer: we continuously assess and measure.

As a lawyer, your performance is constantly being scrutinized by your clients. Every facet of your relationship with them is being assessed. Here is the question: Do you have any input into the ruler by which you are being measured? In other words, to what extent are you able to manage your clients' expectations?

Just as you and I do, most clients create their "evaluation rulers" in their own minds. They decide how to assess you. Unfortunately, much of this assessment is done after the fact and—despite the popularity of the axiom—hindsight is rarely 20-20. Even if your clients were paying close attention during your conduct of their legal matter, when it comes time to pay the bill, they will subjectively reflect backward and—sometimes even with negative overtones—try to measure you in a way that will support a lower fee.

For a number of reasons, you need to forestall such possibilities.

Breaking Down Potential Fees

Your ability to manage client expectations starts by building the ruler together with the client. You need to discuss with them *in advance* such issues as: What will likely happen during the course of this case? What are the variables that can affect a case of this nature? What are the expected time frames? What are the things within your control as a lawyer, and what are the things outside of your control? What challenges might arise that you cannot predict and that your client cannot predict? How would such challenges impact time? How would they impact effort? How would they impact cost? (You may want to note these questions together with any additional ones that come to mind, and use them as a checklist to ensure you don't miss anything when you are managing client expectations.)

Some of you may be thinking at this point, "I can't possibly manage the expectations of my clients so precisely. In litigation, for example, there are just too many uncertainties I would never be able to foresee." Indeed, it is for this reason that some lawyers are afraid to quote their fees.

If you reflect on it, however, you will discover that you *can* be fairly specific in managing client expectations. What you need to do is to break down your work into segments—making each phase as small as necessary. The first phase, for example, might be receiving materials, reviewing them, and having a preliminary discussion with the client about them. Another phase might be the discovery process. Whatever the nature of the work, if you break it down into specific segments, you will find you are able to manage the expectations for that segment.

Reaching Agreement

Once you have built the ruler with the client by going over the variables that could come into play in the matter, and identifying the roadblocks that might come up—some that are probable, some that are less so—your next step must be to make sure that the client is on the same page as you are by asking them to reiterate their understanding.

This is a delicate maneuver. You don't want to sound patronizing. You don't want to sound condescending. You need to say something to your client like, "Now, I just want to be absolutely certain that I have explained adequately how I see the process unfolding. You would do me a great service if you would just give me a quick overview of your understanding, so I can make sure I haven't left anything out."

By doing this, you have created an opportunity to hear the client's perception. You have given yourself an opportunity to fine-tune the perception, and to add to it if necessary. In addition, you have gone a long way toward managing your client's expectations.

Most lawyers fail to help their clients anticipate the potential costs of their legal services. By learning how to manage the expectations of your clients in this area, you will provide yourself with a strong competitive advantage, and you will help to protect yourself from the very negative perceptions that routinely arise against lawyers—especially at the conclusion of cases.

Chapter 11

Building Client Rapport

Have you ever wondered why some lawyers seem to have such a tremendous rapport with their clients? Why they are so trusted? Why they are so highly respected? Why clients are so comfortable dealing with them, and frequently refer other clients to them? Other lawyers seem to struggle. They seem always to be at odds with their clients. They even seem at times to be fighting with them.

In my experience, the difference between lawyers who do have good rapport with clients and those who do not is related to communication, which is the pillar of any relationship. While it is true that you need to treat clients with some professional distance, at the same time you want to establish as much of an affinity with them as you can, so that you have your client on your side.

How do you do that?

Blanket Solutions Don't Work

Some years ago, while I was still practicing law, client satisfaction experts told a seminar of lawyers that we as professionals should project effort to our clients in order to increase client-satisfaction levels. They said that one way to do this was to show the client everything we did. If we were making an appearance in court, for example, we should invite the client to attend, even if the client's presence was not required. We should provide the client with extensive documentation, such as copies of correspondence with the other side—where appropriate, and unless it was very sensitive—just so the client could see the magnitude of the effort we were expending.

The problem with this kind of simplistic approach is that it does not take into consideration the idiosyncrasies of different clients. After this seminar, I began to send one very significant client every piece of paper I could find that was relevant to the case. Several months later, the client told me in no uncertain terms that he was aghast that we would spend so much money to send him documents he did not need to read. I was more than a little surprised to have followed the suggestions of a client-satisfaction seminar, only to have one of my best clients tell me that what I had learned was nonsense.

Our communications must be customized to each individual client. We must get to know each client and get to know the communications needs of that client.

Consider the Client

You should always consider the impact of your communication methods on the potential perceptions of your clients. In some countries, for example, it is still the practice to screen telephone calls—and some people have good and valid reasons for doing so. They say that knowing who is on the other end of the line allows them to get their thoughts together, perhaps to get the file open on their desk before they begin the conversation. If you do screen calls, ensure that your client is left with no hard feelings as a result. If, for example, your secretary asks who is calling *before* telling your client that you are or are not available, you have just potentially offended your client. If your secretary says you are not available *after* learning who is on the line, your client will suspect—even though it may not be true—that you were available until you learned the identity of the caller. It is wise to consider potential client perceptions when determining all of your standard methods of communication.

Tailor Your Approach

As was the case in managing client expectations, one foolproof way of assessing individual client communication needs is to give the client options. Say to him or her, "These are the options available to us in terms of our communications in this matter. We could do A or we could do B. We can involve you in C or we can involve you in D. We can give you these means of communicating with us or those." Let the client choose.

In building client rapport and refining individual communications, it is also important to provide clients with opportunities for feedback. It is extremely valuable to ask your client from time to time such questions as, "Are we keeping you well informed?" "How are our communications with you?" "Are you experiencing any frustrations in communicating with us?" and even, "Are any of the people with whom you work having any frustrations with our firm that they are reporting to you?"

When you receive responses from your clients to these questions, act on them.

Get the Magic Touch

By constantly giving the client good choices in how you will communicate with them, listening to their preferences and acting accordingly, and getting feedback on an ongoing basis, you will begin to build an exemplary kind of relationship with your clients. You will become one of those lawyers who for some "magical" and "mystical" reason clients happen to like. You will become one of those lawyers to whom clients are likely to send referrals. Furthermore, you will have less stress in your practice.

Try it.

Chapter 12

Getting Referrals

Many highly experienced, very capable lawyers believe that if they do quality work for existing clients, word-of-mouth will pave the way to a successful and growing future practice. And yet a study into referrals shows that only about 37 percent of clients refer business to a lawyer with whom they are happy—despite the fact that more than two-thirds would be pleased to do so if they thought the lawyer wanted referrals.

Apparently as lawyers we send out very negative signals—albeit unintentionally—when it comes to attracting new work. A client phones and says, "How are you?" and we say, "Busy. How are you?" Someone asks us, "How is it going?" and we answer, "Well, I was in the office at six this morning, and I'll be lucky to be home at ten tonight." We exude success in our personal lives, and we exude success in our professional lives. As a result, many good clients do not want to bother us. In fact, another study reveals that approximately 18 percent of our clients believe that if they refer a matter to us, we will be *un*happy. We will be sorry they made the referral because we are not in a position to take on new work.

How do we turn this around?

Consider the Roadblocks

There are two obstacles to our getting the referrals we deserve as lawyers:

1. Our clients probably do not know that we desire to receive referrals.

2. As lawyers, we think it is not dignified or appropriate for us to ask for referrals.

I believe that this second obstacle is a "mind-set" problem that emerges from a fundamental fear shared by many lawyers: we are afraid of "looking hungry," afraid of appearing to need work. In our estimation, it is not the badge of a successful lawyer to look hungry: lawyers do not hang around the streets wearing sandwich boards. We have been conditioned to believe that successful lawyers are inundated, successful lawyers are swamped, successful lawyers are so busy that they do not even know the names of their own children. Successful lawyers are so busy they can barely breathe. This is the impression many of us have of the successful lawyer—and we assume it is the impression the public has as well.

Furthermore, we do not want to make our firms look hungry. Especially in well-established firms, many senior people will argue that it is inappropriate to allow the community to believe that a law firm needs work. They feel it sends out a notion that maybe there is something wrong at the firm—that something is not going well—and, of course, sending out a message like that is unacceptable.

Paving the Way for Referrals

So how do you attract referrals without losing dignity? The first step is to learn to acknowledge your right to ask for referrals. You need to identify what kind of referrals you want, and then to determine how best to earn them.

If there are areas of work in which you have special expertise or unique experience or special systems that mean that you can offer better value than other lawyers, then it is quite appropriate for you to seek further work. In asking for those referrals, you should be prepared with reasons that will be satisfactory to a client, so that the client will know that you are not asking because you are not busy enough or because you are hungry or because something is wrong at your firm.

For example, let us say you have recruited some people in a specific legal area, and you are attempting to build a more specialized practice that those individuals can serve. This is a perfectly legitimate reason to go to an existing client and say something like this: "You know the [such-and-so] work we do for you? Well, we love that work and we are building that department. We have recruited some additional people, and we are focusing on trying to get more work of that nature. Given your involvement in your industry, we thought perhaps from time to time you might be asked by other people if you know of a firm that enjoys doing this kind of work, and if that happens we would really appreciate it if you kept us in mind."

There are more aggressive or proactive approaches for seeking referrals that also do not compromise dignity. Visualize a situation where you have targeted a prospective client, and you know that an existing client knows the prospective client and can provide you with an introduction. In this situation you can say to your client something like this: "Would you be comfortable with organizing a lunch that I would be delighted to underwrite, where I could make the acquaintance of your industry colleague [So-and-So]? We would like to act for that person's company at some future time, but I assure you I will not embarrass you by raising the issue directly during the lunch. I would see the subject matter at the lunch itself as being my interest in gaining more industry knowledge, to help me serve you better."

Think of one referral source that could introduce you to a prospective client you would enjoy serving. Use your journal to strategize in bullet-point form how to approach the referral source. After you have had the interaction, note your achievements and next steps. Also note any challenges that you encountered and how you might have prevented them or handled them better. By using your journal on an ongoing basis, you build ever-greater confidence in your ability to execute, and prevent or handle challenges more effectively and with greater ease.

With a reasonable excuse—a real one, mind you, not an invention—and a reasonable approach, you can with dignity and honor ask your existing clients to consider referring others to you, and still maintain your prestige.

Part III

Putting Client-Relations Skills to Work

Chapter 13

Delegating Assignments

In many firms, the process of delegating work has become a vicious, negative cycle. Most of us do not do it well. We do not provide adequate guidance to those to whom we delegate and, as a result, the outcomes are poor or at least unsatisfactory to us. Based on such experiences, we prefer not to try again.

This is a negative cycle that successful lawyers must break. If you want your practice to be profitable, you absolutely must find ways of getting work down to the lowest level of competency. By doing this, you will open yourself to a number of glorious opportunities. Among them:

- You will be able to focus on those aspects of cases or matters that you really enjoy, and that suit your levels of skill and competence;
- you will be able to develop your practice better because you will have more business-development time; and
- you will be able to bring other people along in the firm so that as you build your practice more and more, you can gain profitability through others.

The Principles

There are seven principles of effective delegating. They are as follows:

1. **Get the attention of the person to whom you are delegating.** It is necessary to brief these individuals properly. You need

to give them the appropriate information, and then have a focused discussion with them about what needs to be achieved. This does not require a lot of time, but it cannot be done effectively while in a full gallop on the way to the courthouse. It cannot be done by throwing a file at someone and saying, "Read this and let me know if you have any questions." That is not delegating. Delegating involves a calm, focused discussion, in which there is enough time for you to explain the nature of the case to the other individual.

2. **Provide context**. When delegating, most people tend to say something equivalent to, "Fix the left front tire, please." They neglect to explain what is wrong with the tire, or how the problem is affecting the performance of the vehicle. When we receive results that do not meet our needs, it is usually at least in part because we did not explain what we wanted. When delegating legal work, give those to whom you are delegating a few contextual details—who the client is, for example, what the matter is about, and how the assignment fits into the bigger picture.

3. **Respect those to whom you delegate.** Even if the people to whom you are delegating are very junior lawyers or support staff with no legal training at all, this does not mean they are not smart, or that they do not have ideas, or that they have not done similar work before—perhaps for other people. It is fundamentally important to ask those to whom you delegate what *they* think they can do to enhance the quality of the work they do for you.

4. **Explain the limitations.** If there are limits on resources—perhaps the client is very fee-sensitive or the matter must be kept within a certain scope for other reasons—it is absolutely necessary to communicate that information to the person to whom you are delegating. Otherwise, they may go off and do the very best job they can but at the same time incur much more time and many more resources than you had in mind. When you are unclear about limitations, you set up those to whom you delegate, and yourself, for frustration.

5. **Obtain feedback.** Before concluding the discussion, ask the person to whom you are delegating about their understanding of the matter. There is much to be gained by saying, for example, "I just want to make sure I have touched all of the impor-

tant bases and discussed all of the ingredients. Would you give me an overview of your understanding, to ensure that I've done this well?" The responses you receive to a question like this can be extremely powerful in helping you shape, fine-tune, and generally improve the quality of the assignment.

6. **Set up a pattern for consultation and/or feedback**. There are some situations where the initial delegation is not the end of the matter—where the people to whom you have delegated are likely to require some supervision and feedback from you on an ongoing basis. It is extremely important that when you delegate, you set up a pattern by which you will get feedback—including specific timelines and objectives for the feedback.

7. **Set a deadline or target date**. Some senior people object that when they delegate, the work that has been promised to them does not show up—either on time, or at all. Often this outcome is partly their responsibility, because they did not delineate a specific target date or deadline. They might say, "But I am dealing with professionals who are responsible and accountable. Why can't I just tell them that the matter is 'reasonably time-sensitive'?" While this is certainly possible, results tend to be of a better quality when you are very specific about deadlines.

To summarize, in order to obtain optimum results when delegating, you need to delegate with quality. This means giving specific instructions in a focused, calm way, providing adequate information including a context into which tasks fit, communicating limitations, obtaining input and feedback from those to whom you delegate—based on their understanding of the matter and their experience with similar work—establishing a timeline and a deadline, and setting up a schedule for supervision and feedback.

Following this system for delegating tasks may sound time-consuming, but it actually is not. In the long term, it involves far less time than does ineffective delegation. If you delegate effectively, people will understand what you need them to do. This means you will end up with a higher-quality work product, and less of your time will be required for correcting mistakes and redoing work that could and should have been done properly in the first place.

Chapter 14

Receiving Assignments

Regardless of your level of seniority, there are likely to be times when you are on the receiving end of a delegation—times when you receive assignments from someone else. When I work with groups of lawyers on the topic of delegating and how to improve the quality of delegating, many of them say that they wish the people who gave *them* assignments would take this training, too, because they are so pitifully poor at it.

"These people throw files at us while they are running out the door, saying, 'Come and see me if you have any questions.' Right. Have you ever tried to see someone like that? If you phone them, you go to voicemail and they don't return your calls. If you go to their door there are two secretaries and three clients ahead of you. These are intensely busy people."

We have to assume that individuals like this are never going to sign up for delegation training, and since the people to whom they are delegating are usually junior colleagues, they are not likely to be offered too many direct suggestions on how to improve their delegating skills. Under such circumstances, it is natural for the person to whom the work has been assigned to think, "This is pathetic. I give up. I can never complete this assignment properly. The person who delegated to me is hopeless and always will be, and there is no point trying."

These statements may be true, but they are also cop-outs. If you want to prosper as a lawyer, *you* must be the one who takes charge of adding quality to the interactions that relate to your assignments. You can learn to compensate for the lack of capability of the person who is delegating. If you have not received adequate instruction, you must make it *your* responsibility to change that situation.

Get the Answers You Need

Here is what you can do when you receive an assignment:

- During the initial communication, listen carefully, make notes, and do the best you can to obtain quality instruction.
- Quickly review the information you receive and locate any gaps. Have you been given a context for the work? Have you been given access to adequate information relating to the case? Is it clear whether or not you should speak to the client directly? Is it clear what, if any, resource limitations there may be, in terms of the time you should spend or the disbursements you can incur?
- Ensure that there is a clear arrangement as to when you can follow up with the person who is delegating the matter to you, so that you can give reports to that person or show the work done to date and get some feedback on the quality of your work.

Ask supplementary questions about the components that are missing—immediately if possible, or in a subsequent meeting.

If it is necessary to obtain a subsequent meeting, you may need to put your request for an audience with the person who has delegated the work to you in writing. You do not need to be long-winded. You can simply say, "I would benefit by knowing a little bit more about the context of this situation. Do you have time to meet with me on this? If not, is there anyone else who can help me?"

If necessary, you can also ask specific questions about the matter itself in writing. "I would appreciate your making it clear whether you anticipate my communicating directly with the client or whether you'd rather I have that communication done through you." Or, "Do you have some sense of the kind of time I should be spending on this matter? Should I just simply spend as much time as I need to to do a top-quality job, or are there limits?"

These are the kinds of questions to which you need to know the answers.

Whether you like it or not, when you receive assignments you are going to be measured on the quality of your performance. If the delegation has been poor, this may not appear to be a fair game, but you can compensate for that. You can take the initiative, diplomatically and politely, in order to fill in the communication gaps. As you are doing so, the people who delegate to you may even inadvertently learn a thing or two, and do a better job of assigning work in future.

Your Own Input

The people who delegate to you are not likely to appreciate the benefit to them of getting your ideas and your input, so they are not likely to ask. They may not even be aware of your experience and knowledge in the area at hand, or your creativity. It may not occur to them that you might have ideas that could bring better quality to the matter. *Do not be afraid to offer an idea or suggestion.*

You can say, "You know, I've done some work similar to this before and I have an idea. Should I tell you what that idea is? Would you like to hear it?" Then stop.

Most people—99 out of 100—will say, "Yes, I would like to hear it. What is your idea?" If it turns out you are dealing with someone so close-minded that they say, "No, that's fine, just carry on"—well, talk to a good recruiter.

By taking such steps as those outlined above, you can take responsibility for adding value to the assignments you are given.

"He who asks a question is a fool for a minute; he who does not remains a fool forever."—Ancient Chinese proverb

Chapter 15

Giving Advice

As lawyers, time and time again we encounter situations where people seek our advice. They look to our expertise, our experience, our skill, our wisdom. They ask us questions, and then they ask us to tell them our conclusions.

This is a trap, and it is a trap that must be avoided.

If we do nothing but dispense our wisdom, we place ourselves in a position where we may find ourselves offending our clients, and where our skills are not appreciated to the extent they ought to be.

Understanding What the Client Wants

When clients seek our counsel, what they are looking for, firstly, is someone who has the skill and experience to provide them with competent help in their legal matter. However, they are also looking for someone who understands them well enough to know what an *appropriate* solution to the matter will be for them.

I will never forget the shock and the horror experienced by a very good lawyer in a large firm who was doing some work for a major chain of department stores. There was a claim against the chain and it was for an extremely large sum of money. The lawyer successfully settled the matter for a modest amount—particularly in comparison to the claim. By doing so, however, his firm nearly lost the client.

The problem was that the client did not *want* to settle the matter. The nature of the case was such that they would have gone all the way to the wall to beat the claim. They needed to win it at any cost because they needed to close the floodgates that settling would open to similar litigation.

The lawyer involved in this case was a terrific lawyer in many ways—he understood the relevant legal issues, strategized well, negotiated well, and so on, but what he failed to do was to transcend the technical issues to understand the context, in terms of what the client really wanted to achieve.

That is a pretty extreme example, but every client has needs and every client has wishes and unless we, as lawyers, understand them, we cannot hope to give the right advice or the right counsel.

Involving the Client in the Process

Let us assume, then, that you do understand your client's wishes. You have listened to the client, you understand their situation, you understand their emotion, you understand where they are going, and you have applied listening skills to show them that you understand. You have also managed their expectations so that the ruler against which you are about to be measured will be a fair one.

There is one more step you need to take. You need to offer advice in a manner that recognizes your clients as adults.

In most situations, as lawyers we can think of options or alternatives that the client might take, and in most cases we will feel very strongly that one course of action is far better than others. We will deliberate, we will worry, we may talk to some of our colleagues, and ultimately we will come to a conclusion on a best course of action. We will be tempted to simply impart that conclusion to the client, saying, "I've considered your matter, and you should take Course A."

The problem with this approach is that the client has no ownership of Course A.

Your job at this point is to educate the client, at least to some extent. Your job is to share with the client the kinds of deliberations you have gone through, the kinds of alternatives you see. There is nothing at all wrong with being very forceful in recommending that Alternative A is far better than Alternative B as a course of action, but we insult our clients when we do not allow them to participate at all in that decision.

Most clients are not stupid. Most clients will accept a strong recommendation from counsel they respect. (Indeed, if you have a client who simply refuses to accept your advice, you may wish to consider whether that particular client-lawyer relationship should continue. How can you serve someone who does not have confidence in you?)

In giving advice to clients, not only must you follow the protocol for effective listening and for managing client expectations, you must also ensure that you treat clients like intelligent adults. You need to provide the client with enough information that they can feel that they are involved in the decision-making process. You need to make recommendations in such a way that the client is not insulted, but rather gains the benefit of your strong conviction about the best course of action. Ultimately, you need to gain your instructions from your clients, thereby allowing you to proceed along an appropriate course of action in which the client has ownership.

In addition to improving communications and allowing your client some ownership of the course that you are taking, if you follow these guidelines, you will be much less susceptible to the client's saying at the end of the matter, "I knew we shouldn't have done that. I knew it was stupid. I knew it was wrong. I don't know why I listened to you."

If the client sees that you proceeded in a way with which he or she agreed, the likelihood of that client's being unhappy, even in a losing situation, is far lower.

Chapter 16

Expanding Services: Cross-Selling

The more sessions I have conducted with lawyers regarding the expansion of their firms' services to existing clients, the more misunderstanding I have seen in relation to this subject. The misunderstanding is normally related to mind-set. An adjustment in approach and attitude can dramatically increase your ability to cross-sell—and your comfort level in doing so.

In most firms, cross-selling is presented in terms of its potential to benefit the firm. "How can we find ways of doing other things for our existing clients that will benefit us by allowing us to attract more work and more fees?"

This approach is entirely misconceived. The appropriate attitude to cross-selling is to look at it from the perspective of the client, not from the perspective of the firm. When we think of our own advantage, most of us sound artificially low-key and humble and even (ironically) nonaggressive in pursuing the matter on behalf of the client, but when we think, "The patient needs this medicine" we gather courage. We feel more comfortable moving forward assertively, and it shows in our demeanor.

The issues you should be examining when it comes to cross-selling relate to the needs of your clients. You need to ask yourself:

- "What are we doing for this client now?"
- "What other things could we do that would be of benefit to the client?"

- "In the case of additional matters that would be of *genuine benefit* to the client, do we have the capacity to fulfill the client's needs?"

If the answers we reach with this line of questioning are positive, "cross-selling" becomes not a matter of what is good for *us*, it becomes an obligation *to the client*. We have a professional responsibility to communicate to the client what we could be doing for them that we are not now doing. This is the spirit of effective cross-selling.

If we approach cross-selling merely to build more business, most of us will find we do not have it in us to pull it off. Most professionals are not skilled enough salespeople to simply push services—nor should we be. What good lawyers need to do is to find *real needs* of clients that can be properly met within our firm, and then to focus on communicating those needs in an appropriate way. (I have often seen lawyers ineffectually attempt to cross-sell and then suddenly realize, "Hey, wait a minute. This would actually be of benefit to the client!" Suddenly their enthusiasm rises, their intensity rises, their focus increases, and they find that they can do it.)

Do the Groundwork

In order to successfully expand the line of services your firm is currently offering a client, the first step is to make absolutely certain before you raise the issue that the client is satisfied with the work you are doing for them already. Trying to do something else for an existing client who is unhappy with your work can lead to very unpleasant discussions. Under such circumstances, the client is likely to feel taken for granted, or even abused; at the very least, there is a very subtle resistance that normally makes the discussion much less than satisfying and leaves the lawyer wondering, "What went wrong?"

How you find out whether the client is satisfied depends on your personality. Some lawyers are very direct. They may look a client straight in the eye and say, "You know, we've been doing really good work for you, haven't we? We've won just about everything we've touched for you. I'll bet you're darned grateful!"

The majority will take a far different approach. They may start with questions. "We've done a lot of work for you, Mr. Client," they may say. "I'd like some feedback from you as to how we're doing for you. Have you been satisfied with our work? Have we given you the advice you think you've needed? Have we been responsive? Have you and your associates been happy working with our staff?"

The style and the exact questions are determined by your judgment and depend on your particular circumstances. The important thing is to get the feedback about existing work before you attempt to cross-sell. It goes without saying that if the client is not satisfied, before you continue your efforts to expand your services, you must resolve their concerns. (Other chapters of this book focus on subjects that may be relevant to this topic, such as chapter 18 "Handling Accounts Exceeding Estimates" and chapter 19 "Dealing with Complaints.")

Make the Suggestion

Once you have some assurance that your client is satisfied with your existing or previous work, you can now broach the subject of other legal needs.

You have probably thought about what the client's other legal needs might be and arrived at some preconceived notions. Again, do not simply talk away about what you have decided in advance. Test your notions with the client. Say, for example, "I've been thinking about your situation and wondering whether you ever have problems in [such-and-such an area]?" Or, "I've wondered whether the proposed new legislation relating to [so-and-so] would affect your human resources department . . . and whether that is of any concern to you?"

After you have spoken, listen to the client's response. In some cases, he or she may respond with something of this nature: "I'm not familiar with that proposed legislation, and I would very much appreciate knowing something about how it could impact us."

By listening to the client, you will determine two things:

1) Is the need you anticipated real?
2) Are there other needs that you had not even thought of that could require further services?

Explain How the Client's Needs Can Be Met

The next step is to advise the client of which lawyer or lawyers at your firm can help them meet their additional legal needs, pointing out the experience, competence, and capacity of those lawyers to provide top-quality services with good value. You can say, for example, "I have the privilege of practicing with [Ms. So-and-So] who has extensive experience in the area of [such-and such]." It does not matter if Ms. So-and-So is an associate or a partner, senior to you or junior; if that individual has expertise that would be of benefit to the client, then point out the existence of that expertise within your firm.

Get the Ball Rolling

The next step is to tell the client that if they would like, they can explore this situation without risk. You can say, "Would it make sense for me to set up a short meeting where the three of us could get together? Maybe lunch, something informal, where we could at least broach the subject? No fees involved. It would give you an opportunity to meet Ms. So-and-So, get to know her a little bit and also to reflect further on whether you think this is an area where you do have a concern. Only if you decide that we should be doing something for you will we proceed to a fee-based relationship in that area, and only on a basis you've approved. Does that sound comfortable?"

In cross-selling, if the client does not feel taken for granted, if the client believes that you care about them enough to understand their needs, and if the client is given an option to explore an avenue that might help them to meet newly identified needs *without risk or commitment at the outset*, the likelihood that the client will expand their legal work with you will be dramatically increased.

Before you move on to the next chapter, choose one existing client who we will call "X." Using your journal, record the answers to the following questions:

1. What are we doing for X now?
2. What other things could we do that would be of benefit to X?
3. In the case of additional matters that would be of *genuine benefit* to X, do we have the capacity to fulfill those needs?

Chapter 17

Transferring Clients Within the Firm

If you want to lose clients, one effective way to do so is to become really good at cross-selling, but never to follow up. Hand clients off to other lawyers in your firm, and leave it at that. Do not worry at all about how their relationships are progressing or how the matters you have referred are working out. Listen to your colleagues when they say, "You don't have to look over my shoulder. I know what I am doing."

If you would rather keep clients, it is worthwhile considering very carefully how you make client transfers.

First of all, remember that the relationship with a client is independent of the service for that client. Your client believes that he or she benefits from your competence and/or care. The client has not made that assumption about the person in the firm who has become involved because of cross-selling.

Effective preparation for a client transfer involves discussing the matter with the other lawyer in your firm beforehand. That discussion may be introduced with words such as the following: "We act for Client X. I believe that Client X has a need that you can help them fulfill with quality and value. I have done some preliminary exploration with the client, and I am pretty confident I can set up a meeting. Are you amenable to this idea? Do you have time to work on this case? Is this work you would like to have? Is this a case you would enjoy?" (There is no point in sending work down the hall that your colleagues do not want to do; that will not be a winning strategy for anyone.)

Next, we need to prepare ourselves to be personally unselfish about our relationship with the client. We need to be able to make it clear to clients involved in transfers that if they have any concerns at any point, present or future, they are at liberty to approach either one of the lawyers with whom they are now working in the firm. In other words, if for any reason my client has a concern about me, and if they are comfortable and confident expressing their concern to you, I should be mentally prepared to welcome their openness with you—despite the fact that I did the initial work for them.

There are some firms with reward systems that operate counter to this advice, but successful lawyers will ignore the compensation relationship in favour of making sure clients are well served and happy. I believe that if we want a long-term relationship with a client, it is in our interests and the interests of the client to be unselfish about territorial protection in terms of our individual relationships with them.

The next step is to get the client together with the lawyer to whom you are transferring the matter. This may involve a preliminary discussion without fee, a fairly informal meeting where your (well briefed) colleague can pose a few interesting and appropriate questions that will elicit from the client their thoughts about the matter, along with statements regarding their needs, their perceived needs, and so on. This is an excellent opportunity for your colleague to demonstrate knowledge and expertise, and perhaps present some ideas about how they might serve the client.

Once that discussion has taken place, it may be appropriate to invite the client to take a few days to reflect on the matter and then contact the firm—with the proviso that it is also open for the firm to make contact with the client.

If the client is inclined to use the lawyer you have recommended, it is appropriate to ask your colleague to keep you extremely well informed on how the matter is progressing. You may need to explain to your colleague privately why you need this information; you might point out, for example, that in the spirit of maintaining good client relationships, you do not want to run into that client at a party and be embarrassed by not knowing anything about the status of the matter your office is handling.

When you are able to serve a client in a new area of practice, and when that service involves someone in your office other than yourself, by following some appropriate steps in transferring the client you can avoid one of the greatest dangers that can arise, especially in developing firms—a client who is not happy with the person to whom the matter was delegated and/or feels that they now have no communication channel in the firm. Lawyers in such firms wake up one day to discover that their clients are using some other firm for both the new area of practice *and* the old one.

Chapter 18

Handling Accounts Exceeding Estimates

How many times have you participated in a matter or a file on which you received a printout from administration that caused you to think, "Uh-oh. We've put in more time than I expected," and/or "These disbursements are higher than I thought they would be"? You look at the printout and you know that the client is not going to be thrilled at all.

This is a difficult situation. All of us want to maintain the loyalty and affection of our clients—and most of us assume that confronting them with an account that exceeds the estimate is going to be a relationship breaker.

Some lawyers make a terrible mistake at this juncture. In fact, two mistakes are available, so they can take their choice.

The first mistake is to say nothing to the client, and to write down the account. Lawyers who do that are actually doing themselves the disservice of devaluing their work without giving their clients the opportunity to know what they have done.

The second mistake is to send out an account for the full amount, hoping for the best. We can all visualize lawyers who have done this—fingers in their ears, waiting for the bombs to go off. Their instructions to their secretaries are, "If Client X phones, I've either died or gone on sabbatical. Take your choice but please don't put them through!"

Lawyers in this situation have good reason for concern. Have you ever been surprised by receiving an account from a professional or other service provider that was higher than you thought it was going to be?

Do you remember your reaction? Do you remember your negative emotion? Do you think there is anything that anyone can say to you at that point that is going to make you love that service provider again?

Probably not.

Do the Groundwork

There are certain steps that successful practitioners use effectively to manage situations such as this.

1. Assisted by their support staff, they monitor their cases from a cost perspective right from the beginning.
2. They review all cases to make sure that no wheels are spinning and that no unnecessary work has been done that has added to the cost; if it has, they reduce the account accordingly.
3. If they see the matter exceeding time or disbursement limits, if they possibly can they contact the client and discuss the situation with them.

If these lawyers are satisfied that the work they have done was necessary and it was beneficial, and there was a good reason for not having kept the client informed—perhaps the costs came up suddenly when the client was unreachable, or even if there was simply a failure to communicate—they start communicating with the client right away. They do not write down the account, at least not immediately, nor do they send out an invoice that the client will perceive as unexpectedly high. They contact the client, and they are honest about what happened.

They say, "[Ms. or Mr. Client], in keeping with our efforts to do what we think is in your best interests at all times, we did work of [such-and-such nature] and the following events occurred. We now have work in progress that amounts to [so-and-so] in fees, and disbursements that are [X dollars]. We need you to know about this situation. We need to know whether you are comfortable with our rendering this account."

The next step is to be very quiet. Stop talking. Let the client talk. The next words will determine your success.

Certainly the client may be distressed, and in that case you will need to listen to the client's concerns and deal with whatever issues are raised. Strategies for managing this kind of situation are discussed in the next section. However, there are occasions when silence gains a huge reward, and the reward is the client's saying, "Well, I suppose if it was necessary and I suppose if it benefited us. . . . Yes, by all means go ahead and render the account."

This outcome does occur. It happens with more regularity than most people would guess. In other words, do not give your work away before the client even has a chance to tell you not to do so.

Dealing with Dissatisfaction

The client may be unhappy with what you have told him or her to the point where he or she may say, "Oh, wait a minute. Hold it. No. That causes tremendous problems for me."

If the client is not happy at all about the situation, and possibly even argues strenuously that you ought to reduce the account, you move into a different mode. To get into this mode, you need to have prepared ahead of time. You need to have rehearsed the kinds of resistance you think that this client might offer. You may need to go so far as to write down the points and imagine in written dialogue how you might respond to the client's resistance, or even in some cases role-play the scenario with a sympathetic colleague. By doing this, you will prepare yourself to a certain extent for your discussion with the client.

Note that there is no difference between how you are managing this situation and what you learned in advocacy or negotiating training—you are simply preparing for the eventualities you might need to face. In the case of an unexpectedly large account, the desirable outcome is a negotiation with the client, where you can listen, you can be accommodating, and you can use good judgment to reach an agreement.

Refer to a Higher Authority

In some firms it will be possible and useful to refer the matter to the management committee or the policy board or whatever the appropriate decision-making body is. It can be quite helpful to be able to say to the client, "If it were up to me I would give you the moon because I love serving you, but I do need to run this past the appropriate decision-making body within the firm. I will advocate for you with them, but I do need to take this step and then report back to you."

Such a statement gives you a chance to come back after further internal collaboration or deliberation within your firm—perhaps with an approval or perhaps without one, but at least with a new opportunity to take the issue back to the client for fine-tuning and possible further negotiation.

It cannot be overemphasized that if you have a situation where your work in progress and/or disbursements exceed what you assume the client's comfort zone to be, the worst possible decision is to send out the account without the client's prior approval. By negotiating in advance, by working something out with the client, by communicating, you preclude that unhappy moment where a client opens an envelope, sees an account that is higher than expected, and then has a very negative view of you for the rest of their lives. You need to negotiate in an appropriate way with the client to find a resolution with which both of you can live. Lawyers who can do this successfully have more satisfied clients than those who cannot—and they also make more money.

Chapter 19

Dealing with Complaints

You will notice that there are two separate chapters in this book that talk directly about dealing with dissatisfied clients: the previous one, "Managing Accounts Exceeding Estimates," and this one, "Dealing with Complaints."

As a lawyer and consultant, I have found that in most firms when you mention the word "complaint," it is assumed that you mean a complaint about money. There is, however, a range of other complaints that we may receive as practicing lawyers, from causing delays to failure to provide a needed document or status report—even rudeness on the part of members of our staff. From time to time, most of us receive complaints, whether warranted or not, on a range of issues unrelated to accounts.

It is important to realize that when we receive a complaint, or when our firm receives a complaint, the complaint is about us. It is a very personal moment, and there is a natural tendency in all of us to become defensive. However, becoming defensive is the worst possible thing we can do if we do not want to exacerbate the situation or increase negative emotion on the part of the client. Successful lawyers—those who have phenomenal practices—learn to take complaints in stride. They know how to deal with them.

Make Satisfaction a Priority

While there is a significant difference between what we do as lawyers and what retailers do, in specific areas we can learn important lessons from the world of retail sales. A long time ago, stores learned that the satisfaction of a happy customer is so valuable that it is even worth investing in situations where the customer may not be right.

Imagine that as a thank-you gift for a speaker—an important client, perhaps, who has come to speak at an internal firm function—you have bought a very expensive clock from a high-end store in your city. You present the gift to the client, who opens it in front of the entire firm—and finds inside the box a bunch of broken clock pieces.

After the event, you take the box back to the store and ask to speak to the manager. In a quality store, the manager will typically look at your clock, then say to you, "I am really sorry that this has happened." He or she will ask the clerk to take the broken clock away so you do not need to suffer the sight of it any further. Then the manager will bring out some velvet cloth and place all the clocks they have of a similar kind to the broken clock on the cloth in front of you, for your examination. The manager will say, "Please select the clock that you would enjoy giving this client the most, and we will prepare a letter of apology to accompany it." He or she may even ask, "Do you want this gift-wrapped to take with you, or would you like us to have it delivered by helicopter directly to your client?"

Unfortunately, if most law firms were in charge of this situation, the first response that you as the unhappy customer would receive would be, "You must have broken that clock on the way over to your office from the store. We don't sell them broken." If we protested that we treated the clock very carefully, we would hear, "Then your client must have dropped it when he was opening it. We do not sell broken clocks, and since we do not sell broken clocks, we are certainly not going to replace this one—not without compensation."

The Superior Approach

When we as lawyers receive a complaint, no matter what the complaint is about—and whether it is with or without foundation—there is a series of steps that we can follow to manage the situation. These steps do not require us to cave in or to "sell out" the people with whom we work by suggesting that they are incompetent, careless, or useless.

The first step is to listen—to seek to understand. You may have heard that expression before: "Seek to understand the complaint." You

In dealing with complaints, the most important step is to overcome the propensity to be defensive. Do not react the way human nature tells you to react. Attempt to have an out-of-body experience: let your spirit rise into the heavens, so that you can look down benignly on the situation. Then give the client an opportunity to vent a little, and to explain the problem.

are not capitulating, you are not agreeing with the complaint, you are simply learning—learning what the complaint is, and what the client's emotion is.

Since the person complaining to you believes that an event occurred that wronged him or her, you can also extend conditional empathy without necessarily agreeing to their complaint. You can say, "Yes, if I were in your shoes and I thought someone had wronged me the way I now understand you think that someone has wronged you, I would be angry too."

Remember that somehow this client has come to a point where they believe of you or your firm that something has gone wrong. While it is true that there are a few intellectually dishonest people in the world, most clients deserve the benefit of the doubt. It is important to give them the courtesy of listening to them and understanding them—and of acknowledging that their emotions are legitimate. It is important for them to know that you agree that the emotion they are experiencing is understandable, given what they believe has happened.

After understanding carefully what they believe the facts to be, you should ask for time to investigate. You do not need to request a lot of time, only a few hours perhaps—time to talk to the appropriate people, to gather the appropriate documentation, to have a close look at the situation. Promise the client, "I'll get back to you very quickly. Is that acceptable?"

If possible, and especially in cases where your judgment tells you this is an important client and the complaint could become significant for them, you may wish to offer to go to their premises to discuss the issue: "Would you allow me to have a quick look at this and meet you in your offices? Is there a time late this afternoon that would be convenient for you?" The mere act of taking their concern seriously, promising to investigate it soon, and agreeing to go to their premises instead of staying in yours will in itself project an image of caring that will go a long way toward helping the client overcome the problem.

Most problems involving complaints arise from misunderstandings, and most are not completely black and white; they involve some misconstruction or miscommunication. What you have done by asking for a little time is to create for yourself the opportunity to deal with the issues at hand in a sober and calm environment with a client who now believes of you that you care enough to really listen, you care enough to investigate, and you care enough to make an effort to resolve the problem.

Finding a Solution Together

The best practice in dealing with complaints involves a joint problem-solving approach. Successful lawyers in these situations do not attempt to be wise, brilliant, or inspired. They do not walk into the client's office with a solution in a bag. They know that whatever solution they have devised is simply not going to be good enough—because the client did not participate in inventing it. The client needs to have some role in the creation of the solution, as did the purchaser of the clock in the earlier example, when the manager offered an array of new merchandise to choose from and a choice of delivery methods.

You may begin by offering some options on which you have been reflecting: "Having considered your problem, [Mr. or Ms. Client], it seems to me that there are a few basic approaches we could look at. One would be [altering this], one would be [redoing that], one would be a meeting where we'd consider [such-and-such]. Have you anything to add to that list? Do any other ideas occur to you that I have not thought of?"

If the client has an idea, add it to the list. If the client does not, it does not matter. By asking, you have still involved the client in creating the list. The important thing is to develop options, and once you have done that, you can ask the client to participate in choosing a course of action. You may ask, "Is one of these options more appealing than any other?"

It is true that rather than adding to your list, the client may say, "I don't like any of your options. What I think we ought to do is [something altogether different]." In cases like that, if you can possibly live with some variation of the "solution" now being voiced by your client, you are going to win big time.

There is an adage that goes as follows: "If you complain to an establishment and your complaint is handled splendidly, you do not return to that establishment with the same positive attitude as you had before, you return with a *more* positive attitude."

Listen to your client's complaint, understand it, then ask questions to find out more. Show that you really care, and ultimately look for a jointly derived solution to the problem. Remember that complaints provide you with an opportunity not merely to deal with a problem, but to enhance the lawyer-client relationship.

Chapter 20

Skills Conclusion

Throughout much of the world—in North America, Europe, Australasia, and elsewhere—the law-practice environment has grown increasingly competitive in recent years. Many lawyers hoping to become more effective in this new, more pressurized environment look for easy solutions. "Maybe we should have a brochure," they say. "Maybe we should do some seminars." They are looking for something that is visible, something that makes them feel good because it is a tangible achievement. If they throw some money around, they reason, they will at least be doing something. Unfortunately for them, however, these are not the kinds of actions that of themselves are likely to lead to progress.

Many firms have learned in retrospect that you can have the best promotional materials in the world, but if a relationship with a client or prospective client cannot be established and sustained in a one-on-one situation, a brochure will not help. The "rubber hits the road" at the meeting point between the firm's professionals and its clients or prospective clients. If the professionals are reasonably effective in these interactions, a good brochure can help considerably, but brochures and seminars and other promotional initiatives do not work in isolation.

The client-relations skills that we have examined in the past several chapters are extremely important to your success in the future. There are many signs that the world will become increasingly competitive, not less so, and that the value of lawyers to their clients is evolving. This means that lawyers who are not continually enhancing their value, and the skills to project that value, will be set aside in favor of those who can. By reviewing and reviewing and reviewing client-relations skills and practicing to enhance them, you will attract big dividends.

Keep in mind that many clients have difficulty comparing one practitioner to another, especially when it comes to relative competence. However, they have absolutely no difficulty answering such questions as, "Who do I think has cared about me or my company more?" "Who do I think serves me better?" "Who do I think is more responsive to me?" "Who do I think has gone the extra mile when I have needed them to do that?" By applying the client-relations skills we have discussed in Parts 2 and 3 of this book, you will give the client reason to respond positively to these critical questions.

Underlying Attitudes Are Crucial

Some people look at client-relations skills in a rather jaded and superficial way. They think, "Oh, good. Now I have this package of tricks—they are sort of like cards from a magic store. I can just follow this short set of instructions and I will make people believe things of me which are quite wonderful."

I caution all of us against subversion by that kind of mind-set. "Faking it" never works for very long, if it ever works at all.

It is fundamentally important that we respect our clients, and that we keep in mind that our clients 1) deserve quality, 2) deserve to have their needs fulfilled, and 3) deserve to get good value for their money. If we keep those three premises in mind and then apply client-relations skills in a sincere way, we will win big.

In a similar vein, there is another danger that can arise in applying these client-relations skills. Some lawyers see these skills as a shortcut to quick client satisfaction, a route that saves the energy of providing truly superior value. People with that attitude are few and far between, but they are not going to win—not even when they apply skills such as the ones described in this program. Why not? Because clients *do* deserve quality. They *do* deserve to have services that they really, genuinely need (we are not in business to do surgery on unsuspecting clients who do not know any better than to let us remove "unnecessary" organs). And because clients *do* deserve value (yes, we are allowed to charge fees for our work, even quite significant fees—but only if our work gives *value* to the client).

These three principles

- Clients deserve quality.
- Clients deserve services they need.
- Clients deserve value for their fees.

may seem trite, mundane, even obvious, but if you keep them front and center, if you focus on them, you will be able to put the client-relations skills to use with conviction and effect.

Working From a Client-Based Perspective

I have seen great enthusiasm in the eyes of lawyers who know there really *is* a benefit to the client in what they are doing for them, there really *is* a benefit to the client in doing this additional piece of work, there really *is* a benefit of which the client is not even aware—and if they are able to make the client aware of that benefit, then the client will appreciate the work that has been done for them even more.

That attitude combined with the client-relations skills described in these chapters can give you wonderful results. They can bring you prosperity and they can reduce your stress considerably, because your clients will be much more satisfied. It goes almost without saying that clients who are more satisfied are much less likely to attack you, bicker with you, or even (heaven forbid) sue you.

We have all heard variations of the contrasting stories about the country doctor who left the forceps in Aunt Martha without negative repercussions to his practice because of his track record of coming at two in the morning through the freezing cold to attend to Aunt Martha and his other patients, and the brilliant specialist who graduated from the blue-chip school with an arrogant attitude and was sued a nanosecond after committing one tiny mistake. "Bedside manner." "Client relations." These are approaches that really work.

The client can see conviction in your eyes, and will sense if it is missing. If the sincerity is there, if the underlying belief in providing quality, fulfilling needs, and giving good value is present, and if it is in that spirit that you apply the client-relations skills outlined in this book, you will have the satisfying practice you desire. Your practice will be rewarding to you on many levels because you will have highly satisfied clients who appreciate you, and are willing to pay you the fees that you deserve.

Part IV

Increasing Your Value

Chapter 21

Becoming More Valuable

The professional-service firm management guru David Maister, who has written such acclaimed books as *Managing the Professional Service Firm* and *True Professionalism*, talks about the fundamental importance of looking at our individual value as professionals—today, and into the future.

As professionals, we need to take a realistic look at the world. Thanks to ongoing technological advances, information is available to everyone on a faster and faster basis. By making use of the Internet, medical patients are far more knowledgeable about their diseases than ever before. They have access to the latest research findings, and to worldwide online groups of other people suffering from the same conditions they have, with whom they can compare the effectiveness of prescription drugs and other remedies. Today when patients walk into a physician's office, they are often fully armed. They know all the research studies related to their condition; they know their treatment options; and they know the studies relating to the various drugs and pharmaceuticals available. No longer can the physician simply prescribe what the last drug sales rep through the office suggested a week ago.

Now let us apply what the medical profession is experiencing to the practice of law.

Our clients are also more sophisticated in the area of legal knowledge than they have ever been before, and as time goes on they are going to become increasingly knowledgeable. They are learning more, and they are learning faster. The information that was formerly the exclusive domain of lawyers is now readily available to the public. Today even senior, powerful practitioners are inundated by in-house counsel with requests for precedents, documentation, and other resources. Many firms are building databases to make information available to existing and even prospective clients.

So where does this leave you?

This is where it leaves you—*If your value to clients is identical one year from today to what it is today, you are in great trouble.*

Creating a Strategy

How you go about increasing your value can only be determined by you individually. You will need to reflect on how you can invest in yourself and how you can make yourself more valuable on an ongoing basis.

There are lawyers who will say, "Our firm doesn't really support this kind of activity. They don't support enough professional development." Or, "My firm doesn't really encourage me to learn new methodologies. They don't give me learning time. Since I am pressured to bill, I need to do things I'm already familiar with."

In such situations, you have two choices. You can wait until the firm gets it right, which could take a considerable length of time, or you can be more selfish. You can take the initiative and allocate some time from yourself, for yourself.

You know better than I do how you can best apply that limited amount of time to increasing your value. In your case, it may involve seeking out a mentor in a field in which you aspire to become better. It may mean reading the trade publications for the industry that you wish to serve. It may involve learning certain methodologies—perhaps even using product-generating software—to acquire information on how to produce your legal work product more efficiently and effectively.

The specifics are not important. The message that is of critical importance here is that lawyers who develop a mind-set and an attitude that tells them they must continually work to become more and more valuable, more and more competent, more and more capable in skills that are dynamic, skills that are changing—those are the lawyers who are going to win big.

Asking the Experts: Your Clients

As part of your initiative to increase your value, you can benefit from studying directly the clients you serve or aspire to serve. Their industries are likely to be changing, too. Find out what is new in the industries with which you would like to work. Talk to the people in those industries. You may get some tremendous ideas for how you can assist these industries by thinking about their future needs.

You can be quite open with such investigations. One law firm I worked with invited several significant clients from a number of different industries to speak to the lawyers in the firm about what was going on in their industries, and what their future needs might look like. It was simply amazing how much everyone learned in just two or three hours from inviting in those client guests.

The learning situation does not need to involve a formal presentation—it can take place at an informal breakfast or lunch. You may wish to form an ongoing group to pursue ideas, and include representatives from several disciplines. You can take one or a myriad of approaches. The important point is to pause and reflect on how you can enhance your value—and then create your strategy.

In some of the most prominent firms on this earth, you either improve or you are out. The world-renowned consulting firm McKinsey & Company, for example, has a "two-year up or out" strategy. When members of that firm get together for a meeting, it is expected that each of them will be able to speak about what they have learned since they last met that would be of benefit to their peers in their practices. This may sound intimidating—and the approach is not for everyone—but it *is* a winning attitude when it comes to improving value.

On a personal practice level, you need to create a plan that becomes your plan for improving, for becoming more valuable. Not very many lawyers are doing this, but those who are doing it soon leave the others in the dust.

(If you turn to the next chapter without making a journal entry, then you will have increased your awareness but not realized any competitive advantage. Make a note of what your plan is; it does not have to be elaborate—simple is fine. And remember the Mount Everest Syndrome: make sure you identify the incremental steps.)

Chapter 22

Lawyer or Consultant?

There is one significant gap in the training that we as lawyers traditionally receive from our educators, and it relates to the conduct of our law practices.

Do law schools teach us how to conduct our practices? I don't think so. In most cases, law schools teach us exclusively how to be lawyers. They teach us to know the law, and they teach us to be learned in the law. The dean of my law school made it clear that he thought it was the job of the firms to teach us how to practice law.

Well, what about the firms? Do they teach us how to practice law? Again, in most cases, no; not formally. If we are fortunate, we get to watch some magnificent practitioners who are very gifted in their areas of practice, and if we gain enough exposure perhaps we can emulate their behavior and learn from them. But in most firms there is no consistent, intense program to help us become better practitioners.

Defining Our Roles

If I were to ask you, "What do you do for a living?" depending where in the world you live you would likely respond by saying that you were "an attorney," or "a solicitor," or "a barrister," or "a lawyer." But what does that mean? Think about it. What do you *really* do when you are practicing the law?

Today, as we look at the advent of multidisciplinary firms and the trend in what we used to think of as large accounting firms to become "full professional service firms," it is a valuable exercise to give close examination to what we really do to earn a living as legal practitioners.

In fact, what a lawyer, or barrister, or solicitor, or attorney actually does is to *consult*. What you really are is a *consultant*. You are a highly specialized consultant, to be sure: a consultant in respect of the law. You are learned in the law; you have studied the law. You are a consultant who helps people apply the law to practical day-to-day situations.

So let us examine good consulting practice. What does a consultant do?

First, a consultant knows how to come into a situation and really listen. By listening, a good consultant reaches a solid understanding of what the problem is.

After listening and understanding, the consultant proposes methodologies that can be brought to bear to resolve the problem that has been identified. In the case of the law, the resolution involves accomplishing a mission—merging two companies, for example. Sometimes the problem is getting cost out of something: How can we save money in the future in dealing with this or that kind of situation? The problem might even be risk management: How can we reduce the chances of being sued, or at least limit the amount of our exposure in the event that we are sued?

In regard to your role in resolving such problems, ask yourself the following questions, and then answer them honestly:

- Do my clients see me as a consultant?
- Do my clients value my counsel?
- Do my clients seek out my counsel?

Adding Value

Rather than as consultant or counsellor, your clients may see you more as a technician. They have found a piece of property they want to purchase, and you are a property lawyer, so they retain you to obtain a title; they are being sued by somebody and they have to defend themselves, so they hire you because you are a litigator and are therefore able to defend them.

I used to tell the articling students hired by our firm that what we do as lawyers is to shine shoes. I said that the shoes we shine are usually quite expensive, and they must be treated extremely well, and the job we need to do must be superlative, but basically we are in the business of shining shoes. I then explained that the message I was trying to convey was that every single one of our clients had options. They had choices. On any given day they could hire some other firm. I was telling them that clients *deserve* and *demand* service—and they tolerate firms that do not understand that only when they have no choice.

Very few law firms anywhere have captive clients who have no choice. And to me, this means that *we need to earn the right to serve every client every day*. The way we do that is by being more valuable to our clients than they expect us to be. We can learn specific ways to accomplish this objective by studying outstanding consultants.

Consultants Who Add Value

You can accelerate your rate of progress toward the kind of practice that you aspire to have by implementing what consultants in other fields have learned about becoming more valuable to their clients. This may involve spending some time with a client with the meter off, just to learn more about their business. It may mean suggesting added-value services like attending their board meetings or strategy sessions to see if there is some preventative advice you can offer.

Many professionals are invited to sit on corporate boards and are invited to strategic meetings, but more and more in recent years lawyers are noticeably and conspicuously absent from such sessions. That has not been the case historically. The founder of one particular firm, a very prominent firm with blue-chip clients, talks about how his father used to go out in a horse-drawn carriage to deliver liquor when one of his flagship clients, a brewery, first began its operations. Now that liquor company is one of the planet's mega-corporations, and is still a client of that law firm.

I suspect that today, many a junior or up-and-coming lawyer would think it was beneath his or her dignity to sit on a wagon next to a young president delivering the liquor for his newly established company. The founders of great firms knew that getting close to the client, being willing to really serve the client, would ultimately give them the kind of practice they desired.

I believe we can help our clients achieve the objectives they have set for themselves, rather than simply helping them to resolve any legal problems that arise. If we can do that effectively then we will be perceived as far more than technicians. We will be perceived as trusted members of our clients' teams. I believe that making significant contributions to the lives of our clients will catapult us forward to attain the kinds of practices we dream of having, despite how difficult and competitive the years ahead may be.

Chapter 23

Doing More Than Required

If you practice law in a firm of any size at all, then you likely experience situations that challenge your patience and intelligence on a regular basis. You are probably, for example, not over-appreciated at your office. You probably do not go in to work in the morning and say, "Please, you've just got to lower the appreciation level around here, because it is going to my head. You applaud when I walk in in the morning, then at lunch the most senior people in the firm compliment my drafting abilities in front of everyone and tell me I have inspired everybody in the firm. . . . This is getting embarrassing."

Not too many people are suffering from that kind of problem.

In most firms, not only are you not getting the appreciation you deserve, you are also not getting the encouragement you need to be innovative or creative when it comes to the application of new information, new methodologies, and new systems for cost saving. You are not being encouraged to learn the newer software and the newer procedures, or to take the time to read in the areas of your clients' industries. In most firms, candidly, what most lawyers are encouraged to do is to bill. They are asked to record hours, to get realizable rates, and to get revenue in the door. That is likely what you are being encouraged to do at your firm.

Even if you do have a few people in the firm who are wise enough and progressive enough to encourage you to do a few other things that might have a bearing on your future, then there are probably some other people with power who make it very difficult for you to do that. You organize an internal continuing education meeting and someone senior says, "Why aren't you working on my brief? Why aren't you working on my case?"

As a result of these kinds of challenges, when we get home at about 8 P.M. we start off the evening by throwing out questions to our significant other like, "Have I been home even once before 8 o'clock this month?" and "Do you know what [X] had the nerve to say to me today?" At that point, our significant other may hand us a drink and give us fifteen minutes to cool off before dinner.

Answer this question: If you had a team that you wanted to perform at peak, whether a sports team or any other kind of team, would you consider it likely that its members could turn in a best performance in a state of mind where they needed an anaesthetic before they could sit down to dinner with their families? I don't think so.

If you are in a firm like the one I have described, you have many challenges, but if you wait until the firm gets it right, you will be very old—or dead—before you accomplish some of the things that you need to do to be prosperous and satisfied. The distinction between winners and losers is very simple. The winning attitude is to accomplish *in spite* of your environment.

Go the Extra Mile

First and foremost you need to get into the habit of doing more than is expected of you—both for your clients and for your firm.

Ask yourself this question, "When is the last time I surprised the people with whom I practice by doing something that went well beyond their expectations?" Ask yourself the same question in relation to your clients: "When is the last time that a client was absolutely amazed because of something I did that was totally unexpected?" For many lawyers, that kind of scenario has not happened recently.

Pause here and think for a moment. Write down a few ways you might achieve the unexpected on behalf of your firm and your clients in your notebook or journal. Think of one or two ways in each area— even little ways, to start.

It is true that there are practical limitations to the time you can devote to such enterprises, given the pressures of multiple tasks, multiple clients, multiple people in the office for whom you need to do things. You work in a messy, intense world. However, this is no excuse for you to do anything less than your best. In fact, you are better off refusing some work than doing less than your best. No one will ever thank you for mediocrity; they will blame you for it instead, and it will not be an adequate excuse that you were overworked.

Whenever necessary, you need to prevent yourself from being swamped with jobs that will impede your ability to do top-quality work. Saying "No" can be a very difficult thing to do—so difficult that in this book, a whole chapter is devoted to doing it effectively. However, that is what you need to do.

The Rationale

Why is it essential that we continuously improve our quality and continuously improve our client satisfaction and continuously improve the satisfaction of those with whom we practice? The reason may be obvious to some, but in my experience it is not obvious to everyone. We do not do it only for the sake of those clients or those fellow practitioners. It is not about doing just anything for the sake of pleasing, and it is certainly not about developing the kind of attitude or personality that is addicted to pleasing other people. What improving our work is about is this: in an increasingly competitive future, the prosperous lawyers will be those who have acquired the skills that allow them to please their clients *at will*.

Professional management expert David Maister tells a story of his early years as a professor at the Harvard Business School. He went to one of the senior members of the faculty and said, "Tell me, how does one get ahead here? What's expected of a professor here at the Harvard Business School?" The answer—which is highly relevant to the topic of "doing more than required"—was this: "David, if the whole world wants you, we will want you. And if the whole world doesn't want you, we won't want you either."

The reason why we need to surpass the expectations of our clients, the reason why we need to surpass the expectations of those with whom we work, is because by doing so we will continue to improve our value and the quality of the work we do. And as times become more competitive and more challenging, as knowledge becomes outdated ever faster, it will be those professionals who know how to do that who will not only survive, but thrive.

Chapter 24

Practice with Courage

An experience that occurred in my very first year of practice taught me a lesson I have never forgotten.

A client called at about 3 o'clock in the afternoon, and he wanted something done by 4:30 that same day. I had no idea how I could get it done in that time period; in fact, I was really quite worried about it. So I went down the hall and I was lucky enough to find the managing partner—quite a brilliant man—and I talked to him about it.

He looked at me and said, "Will someone die if this doesn't happen by 4:30 today?"

"Well, no," I said. "Of course not. No one will die. This is just a routine legal issue, not death row stuff."

He said, "Well then, I doubt it has to be done by 4:30, does it?"

As I paused and reflected on that, he guided me further. He said, "You really have to be realistic about how long things take. You really have to educate clients as to the time you need to do things well for them, and you need to have some kind of reasonable rapport with clients about the time frames they will allow."

The Courage of Your Convictions

How many times have you experienced pressures that resulted from situations where you wanted to be accommodating, whether it was to a senior in-house counsel for a large corporate client, or to an individual? Newer lawyers may be more susceptible to this than more established ones, but most of us have experienced this kind of pressure at some point—some more often than others.

In order to have a successful practice, we need to muster some courage. That courage manifests itself in our willingness to be straight with our clients, and to counsel them the way we think we should. It is important and appropriate that we have the courage to tell our clients at times even those things that they do not want to hear.

When we are new in the practice of law we are horrified by the thought of being completely straightforward. What if we offend the client? What if the client becomes unhappy? What if—heaven forbid—the client seeks other advice?

Based on the best practices I have seen, I can assure you that the most successful practitioners are willing to be candid with their clients. They are willing to counsel them frankly and the result, much more often than not, is a deepened respect on the part of the client for the lawyer.

It is true that we walk a fine line here, and judgment is required. In earlier chapters we explored—especially in the context of client relations—the importance of listening, the importance of understanding, the importance of not having preconceived notions about what everybody else should do and simply delivering those notions in a bag. We talked about how to give advice that includes options and other mechanisms that allow the client to appreciate and take ownership of decisions regarding their legal matters. Now, on the other side of the coin, I am warning against a propensity to be accommodating to an extent that means we do not speak with a real conviction to the client.

There are too often times when we tell the client what the client wants to hear. As a result, a little later in the process we admonish ourselves. We say, "Why wasn't I a little more courageous? I knew this would happen. I was worried about this course of action. Why did I let the client bully me into what I believed to be an inferior course on this case?"

The tension between being receptive on the one hand and standing up for your convictions on the other must be resolved initially by listening well, understanding well, being open to ideas—especially from the client—and being amenable to reconsidering your position and/or your suggestions or recommendations. However, when you believe deeply that the client is asking you to make a mistake on their behalf, you need to stand up and let that be known. You can do it politely, but you need to do it with courage. Many more clients will respect you and will appreciate you than not for this behavior.

Some of the great business leaders alive today say, "If I have someone in my organization who always agrees with me, one of the two of us has to go." If all you ever do is agree with your client, you will be of little value to them because you will find yourself steering them along a dangerous path.

It is an enormous challenge to practice with courage. You must balance concerns about offending the client with the need to tell them what you believe deeply—and you must know how to tell them straight, but also diplomatically. When you use this skill judiciously, your clients will appreciate it—and you will prosper for it.

Chapter 25

Leadership Styles

Whether you are a sole practitioner, the head of a practice group or an industry group, or lead a client team, there are times when you will need to exhibit the attributes of leadership.

What do leaders really do? Leaders provide direction for a group or team of people so that they have some idea where they are going. Leaders also find ways to get good levels of performance from the individuals who comprise the team.

A brief examination of four different styles of leadership will enable you to think through what style or combination of styles might work best for you, given your situation.

1. The Dictator

Dictators give orders, and other people are supposed to simply follow them. Needless to say, this leadership approach will rarely work in a law firm environment, primarily because of the attributes of the people who constitute such firms. As we mentioned earlier in this book, lawyers are typically ferociously independent, and they have a propensity to be quite analytical and critical. (Again, these are not insults, but rather descriptions of the attributes of a good and strong lawyer.) Although all lawyers need to suspend their predispositions to be independent, analytical, and critical from time to time if they want to be innovative and creative, these are natural attributes in most cases. As a leader, you really need to take them into consideration.

121

I have seen the dictatorial approach work only once in a law firm, and it was a rather exceptional situation. The leader of one of the mega-firms also founded a bank at the same time as he built this large and successful firm, and during a recession when most of the banks in his part of the world went broke, his did not. He was very strong indeed, and very successful. The dictatorial approach worked for him; he gave orders, and other people followed them. (He was also a little idiosyncratic. He banned coffee from his offices, for example. He did not have religious objections to coffee; he just thought that taking coffee breaks was the wrong thing to do. So he had a rule in his firm: no coffee breaks and therefore no coffee. It was quite amazing to hear senior, powerful litigation partners explain how they used to sneak out the back door of their office tower and around to the side door of the office tower next door, just to get a cup of coffee.)

While the dictatorial approach worked for this man, it is very rarely effective in law firm settings.

2. The Visionary

The visionary leader is someone who sees a picture in their mind of what the group can achieve, and is able to convey that picture to the group in such a way that individuals within the team aspire toward the same result. Some people can pull this off—they are rare, but they do exist. In my consulting work throughout the world, I have seen two firms where the leaders are so strong and so well respected in this regard that when people talk about them behind their backs, they are actually saying positive things. It is really quite amazing when it happens, but success using this approach to leadership exclusively is uncommon.

3. The Role Model

A third style of leadership is that of role model. In this situation, the leader is so strong in their own personal performance that others around them simply aspire to match that performance, or at least are willing to try to match that performance. This is a potentially dangerous leadership style if it is used exclusively, due to the tendency of human beings to differentiate themselves in some way from a leader. They may see themselves as having a different preference of lifestyle from the leader, or as having a different character or nature, or perhaps they believe that they do not have the capacity or the talent that the great leader has. And so they separate themselves from that individual, and his or her effectiveness as a leader is diminished as a result.

4. The Coach

The fourth style of leadership is that of a coach. What do coaches do? Coaches help others improve their performances.

Coaches may operate with considerable subtlety, acting as effective catalysts to help individuals reach their peak performances. Good coaches hold up a mirror of honesty to those they coach, discouraging self-deception. They also offer options beyond those currently under consideration by those who are being coached.

Your Leadership Style

Good leaders demonstrate pieces or parts of all the styles described above. There are times—during a crisis, for example—when all leaders need to be dictatorial. They need to give orders, and for a while people need to follow those orders. From time to time all leaders, either individually or with their groups, need to paint a picture of what the group should aspire to do, so that the group can move in a particular direction. (This subject is discussed in more detail in Chapter 26, "Meetings Worth Attending.")

Leaders also must demonstrate some role modeling. By way of a case in point, many law firms have tried to create leaders out of people who have never really practiced law, or do not currently practice law, and the result can be a real struggle because of the inability of that person to act as a role model. Whether or not we are right to do so, it seems that most of us as lawyers will only follow a leader who we think either has practiced law very well or is at least capable of doing so. Therefore, most leaders need to exhibit some practice prowess. Most of the managing partners, even in the mega-firms, continue to practice some of the time or have had exemplary practices.

As discussed above, role modeling is a dangerous style if it is used exclusively, because some people may wish to distance themselves from you and not want to follow you. Nonetheless, it can be effective as a component of your leadership behavior if it is used carefully. You need to remember that your behavior speaks more loudly than your words;

you need to behave in a manner consistent with the message you are trying to send. This does not mean you have to be the top biller or attract the most clients to the firm, but it does mean that you have to put in an effort in the areas you think are important for others to emulate.

An expression that comes to mind in this regard is one you have no doubt heard before: "Your behavior is so loud that I can't hear what you are saying." There are many leaders of law firms who say they aspire to certain things, but if you watch their performances, they do not behave congruently with their statements. For example, some senior people who want junior lawyers to enhance their skills in a particular area will organize a meeting and bring in a guest speaker for those juniors, then when the meeting starts the senior person will look at his or her watch and say, "Now, I have to leave, but this is very important for you and I think you should stay until the end."

What is the message here? The message is that despite having organized this meeting, the senior person actually feels the issue is trivial—suitable for junior people but not for serious lawyers. As a leader, you need to be very concerned about your behavior. It often broadcasts your beliefs far more strongly than do your words.

The Coaching Style

Given the independent nature of the people that you are leading, the coaching style of leadership can offer the best hope of success. Your goal here will be to capture a spark that is within the members of your team, a spark that is consistent with a dream *they* have—that is consistent with *their* aspirations. In order to tap into that spark, it is necessary to gain their trust, and then to be a catalyst for their performance.

From a practical point of view, to make this happen you need first to spend some one-on-one time with the people you are leading, getting to know them personally and professionally. You need to learn what their values are, what kinds of things they like to do, what their families are like. You can ask them questions about their law practices such as the following:

- What led them to choose the career they have—why did they study law?
- What kind of practitioner would they like to become?
- In a perfect world, what area of expertise would they choose to have?

- If they could have the career of their dreams, what would separate them from other lawyers? What would distinguish them? What would be special about them?

Using What You Learn

Make certain that you keep notes on those personal discussions. It may be wise to make those notes privately after the discussion is over, as some people may find it disconcerting if you do it visibly; they may worry that you are evaluating them. Referencing these notes over time will prove immensely valuable as you can then track changes that might not have been obvious otherwise.

By understanding the goals and dreams of those around you, you achieve a number of quite remarkable things. First of all, you can begin to deploy people where you have tasks that fit with their aspirations. Imagine, for example, that you need assistance with a tedious research project. It may sound trite and it may sound obvious but it does not happen often enough—if you can choose someone to do the work who aspires to be an expert in an area consistent with the research, that person is likely to be far more willing and happy to do the work than someone with no interest in the field. The latter may do it begrudgingly and only, really, because they have been asked to do so.

Secondly, if someone believes of you that you genuinely care about them and that you are genuinely attempting to help them achieve the kind of career that they would like to have for themselves, then they will do more for you. If they believe of you that you are genuinely supporting their career aspirations, and if you occasionally say, "Go along with me just this one time and help me out on this project" or "Help the team out on this project," they are likely to give you the help you need, and to do so willingly.

In summary, in terms of leadership styles, you are likely to get your biggest return for the time you invest by coaching those around you. In many of the very best law firms in the world the leaders do not stand out as dictators, they do not stand out as visionaries, they do not even stand out as role models. They stand out in subtle ways as people who quietly and appropriately intermingle with their people, acting as a catalyst, assisting and endeavoring to increase and enhance the performance of individuals and teams on an ongoing basis. These are the heroes: the people who can improve a firm over time, and do it almost invisibly.

Chapter 26

Meetings Worth Attending

How do the people in your firm feel about meetings?

Based on my observations of many, many law firms, I can guess.

Let us begin by ranking meeting-appreciation scores on a scale of 1 to 10, where 10 means "I love meetings. Meetings in my firm are inspirational, personally and professionally. I wouldn't miss one. I always get there early, always leave late. I love them." At the other end of the scale, the number 1 represents a view that meetings are attended out of duty and obligation. People who feel this way, if given a choice, would not show up at all at meetings: they are there simply to be perceived as a team member. They usually sneak in files to work on while the meeting is going on, and they probably have a cell phone that they are able to set to vibrate instead of ring.

In most firms, there are far more people at the "1" end of the meeting appreciation scale than there are anywhere near the "10." Why is that? I believe it is because most people do not perceive that the meetings they attend have much value to them as individuals. They go to meetings out of a sense of obligation, but they do not believe they really get very much out of them.

The Preliminary Steps

If you want to put on meetings that people want to attend and participate in, there are some preliminary steps you need to take with your group. First, you need to get the group together and ask this question (and you need to be willing to accept the answer): "Is there anything that can be accomplished by this group of people acting together that we cannot accomplish alone?"

This is a fundamentally important question. If the answer is "No," then why in the world would you want to have a meeting?

In most cases, however, when practice groups or industry groups or client groups or production teams are brought together, they find that there *are* things the group can accomplish that individuals cannot achieve on their own. The members of your team are probably smart, and if you give them the opportunity to identify a number of things they can accomplish together that they could not accomplish alone, it will take them only a few seconds to do so.

The next step is to allow them to prioritize those things. What is the most important part? Where is the greatest potential yield? What is the least important part? If they could do without something on their list, or something they usually do in meetings together, what would it be?

The next step is for you to make a contract with your group. Your contract as leader is this: "If I promise to keep us focused on those things that we have collectively decided would be of the greatest value to us, then are you prepared to attend meetings?" This is the deal you need to offer.

The best leaders get feedback from members of the group on an on-going basis as to whether the meetings continue to have value. If they do not, they fine-tune the nature of the meetings so that they do once again.

Setting Guidelines

Let us go to the conduct of the meetings themselves.

We all know the basic rules for meetings—for example, that an agenda is useful so that everyone knows what is intended to be achieved. It is also helpful to have a starting time and an ending time.

In regard to starting and ending times, many people say, "I think everybody knows that it's important to have those." Well, if everybody knows it, why are they not doing it? Why do meetings start twelve minutes late as a rule in most law firms on this planet? Why do people saunter in and out from time to time? It seems that the excuse, "Well, I was on the phone with a client," or "I was at a client's office," or something similar is a bullet-proof excuse in law firms, allowing people to waltz in whenever they feel like it.

What I observe happening at the beginning of most meetings is, in fact, a kind of dance. A senior person will walk in at 12 o'clock sharp, the time for which the meeting was called, look around, see no one junior present, and decide, "I'll make another phone call. I'm not sitting here waiting for junior people." At 12:01, a junior person walks in and says, "There's no power here. I can go and make another phone call and not get into any trouble." And so on. People go in and out of the room until somehow a critical mass forms and then they begin to stay. In a time-oriented environment like a law firm, this is not a productive use of time or people.

So what is the way around it?

Here is some good news. When I have talked seriously to people in such situations and said, "Why do you do that? Why do you waste so much time? Why do you saunter in late? Why do you leave early?" the answer is typically this, "I do it because everybody else does. I used to come on time but it was of no benefit. Meetings never start on time around here."

Here is more good news. If you address this issue with your group, if you ask the group to identify, individually and collectively, the kinds of rules that they think would be appropriate by which they would like to be governed, they will very quickly come up with objectives that include such items as "starting meetings on time" and "finishing meetings on time."

You need to go one step further. You need to ask the members of your group, "How will we make this happen? How can we enforce a rule like that? Perhaps with some humor, perhaps with some fun? Should we have some polite sanctions for those who don't follow our group rules?" I have seen otherwise serious lawyers come up with ideas like hats that were specially made for anyone to wear who was late for a meeting, or the imposition of fines, or—conversely—a special coffee that is ordered for everyone who arrives at the meeting on time but not for those who arrive late.

Some of these ideas may sound silly as you read them here, or inappropriate, but the point is not what you think. It is not up to you as a leader to set the rules. If you do—if you decide on some sanctions and you attempt to impose them—you will soon have a revolt on your hands. If you belong to any clubs, you will know that the rules of a club are enforced by the members, not the leader. No one says, "We'd better call the president of the club at home. Somebody is smoking in the non-smoking area." That is not the way it works. Members enforce the rules. Therefore, in a fun way, allow your group to set its own sanctions. Once your team has set some sensible rules, if someone breaks them, the sanctions will come automatically from others in the group—and your leadership role will be far easier.

Moving Toward Action

Now that you have people meeting, now that you have them following some reasonable rules that they have established, you need to focus on the most important reason for meeting at all, and that is to decide on some appropriate actions that the group might take that might move it forward. Earlier in this book when we discussed creating a personal plan for yourself, we indicated how you could select some alternative actions that might be appropriate for you, and then choose one or maybe two from your list that you thought would have the highest yield. The same approach exactly applies to the group.

Once the issues where action may be appropriate have been decided, you can involve the group in brainstorming. In order to do that, you will need to explain the brainstorming rules to your group. Once again, as set out in Chapter 2, those rules are:

1. Say and write down everything that comes to mind. In group settings, you will need a flip chart or a dry-erase board so that everyone can see the points as they are recorded, and you will need a volunteer to be the scribe.
2. No discussion is allowed. The goal is to develop a list of alternatives as quickly as possible. They will be analyzed later.
3. No value judgments, positive or negative. No one gets to say, "Good idea" or "That will never work." Value judgments impede creativity.
4. Record all ideas—everyone's ideas. Failing to record an idea sends a negative message to the originator of the idea.
5. Piggybacking on ideas is not only desirable but is encouraged. Remember that it is the nature of a brainstorming activity that apparently stupid or ridiculous ideas can lead to brilliant ones.

With those rules, written down if necessary, have your group generate a list of possible specific actions that would move the group toward its defined objective. By way of example, let us imagine that an industry group in your firm decides that it wants the firm to be more appealing to a specific group of target or prospective clients. The group might want to brainstorm on possible actions under a phrase such as, "In order to be perceived as a better alternative to our described target clients, we could do . . . what?" Now the group brainstorms specific actions.

Again, you as leader need to make sure that the actions that go onto the list are specific—generalities will not work. "Raise our profile" is not an action, for example. That is a concept. So if someone in your group suggests "Raise our profile," you as leader need to ask, "What might we do to raise our profile? What do you have in mind? Can you illustrate that? Can you give me a couple of examples of what we might do to raise our profile so that we have more specific actions?"

Although the rules do not allow discussion while the brainstorming is taking place, you are not breaking the brainstorming rules when you as a leader help the group in terms of process. Debating the merits of ideas at this stage is not permitted, but asking people to be more specific about their actions is appropriate. By doing so, you are helping them to develop a menu of alternative actions.

Once the group has created its menu, you need to facilitate the group in setting its priorities. Let the group scrutinize the list and then canvass the group. What are the most widely acceptable ideas? For which few ideas is there the most enthusiasm?

Finally, you need to find out whether there are people in your group who will volunteer to actually carry out some of those actions. This is a critical moment. If, in considering a point, everyone sits with arms folded looking at you—or, indeed, looking away from you—put a big line through that item on the list. "Let's not deceive ourselves," you can explain. "If none of us has the impetus to want to do this, then why leave it on the list? It isn't going to happen."

There are times when I have watched groups pause when that line is drawn, and someone will say, "But wait. We've got to do that one! It's extremely important." At that point, you can return to the question, "Well, if it's so important, is there anyone willing to participate?"

You may or may not get a volunteer at that stage. The important thing, though, is to look for those actions that have wide support and with respect to which people have some intensity, because those are the actions that will get accomplished. Those are the actions that will move you forward.

To encapsulate, then, meetings worth attending involve the following components:

- Ensuring that the group sees some merit in getting together—that its members realize what they can accomplish together that they cannot accomplish alone;
- Allowing the group to set some sensible guidelines. What are the rules of engagement? Do they want meetings to start on time and end on time? What else do they want to see?
- Running meetings in accordance with what the group has decided it wants, following the pattern that has been agreed upon in terms of starting and finishing meetings, and keeping the meeting focused on important subjects;
- Ensuring that meetings are action-oriented. A meeting should never end without an answer to these questions: "As a result of our deliberations, are there any actions that would be appropriate for us to take?" and "If indeed there are some appropriate actions, are there any for which we have enough enthusiasm, that we think would have enough reward, that we are actually prepared to roll up our sleeves and use some of our very scarce and precious nonbillable time to achieve them?"

If you follow this pattern with your group you will not only have productive meetings, you will have meetings that people want to attend. Participants appreciate such meetings because they can see that they derive a benefit from being in attendance.

Chapter 27

Overcoming Meeting Challenges

Some very difficult and challenging situations can arise during meetings involving lawyers. In no other setting are the propensities to be "ferociously independent" and "critical and analytical" more obvious. In my experience, as soon as an idea is about 18 inches out of one partner's mouth, another is drawing a sword and slashing straight through it.

Why does this behavior exist? Are these lawyers mean-spirited, horrible people? Absolutely not. They do this because they are so gifted at seeing issues from so many perspectives that once they see an idea spinning to the left, they cannot resist demonstrating to the group how the same idea would look if it were spinning to the right.

Agreeing to Take Different Approaches

As the leader of a meeting, you are likely to find situations where the minute someone has an idea—let us say the idea is "orange"—someone else will immediately say "apple," and away they will go. Because of their advocacy experience and because of the nature of lawyering, they will tend to polarize. The orange person will begin to discuss the attributes of oranges, the apple person will begin to defend the attributes of apples. They will begin to debate, then a few of the other people around the table who have political loyalties to one or the other will get into the fray. Before you know it, there will be a real team-against-team approach occurring in the meeting. This kind of activity is completely counterproductive. It is a waste of time.

In order to deal productively with situations like this, you need to keep in mind that different ideas can coexist. We tend to have a notion that everyone in a group must agree on everything, but this is not true; different people can do different things in different ways.

I recall a practice group meeting where Lawyer A stated that that he did not believe in having lunch with prospective clients. He thought it was wrong to do that. Lawyer A decided to profess that luncheons with prospective clients were inappropriate. Within a nanosecond Lawyer B said, "I have developed some of my best clients by taking people for lunch. I think it's a terrific tool." The debate began.

After a few moments, the leader said, "Lawyer A, I appreciate that you don't like the approach from your own perspective, but do you have any problem if B goes for lunch with his prospective clients?" And Lawyer A said, "No."

And then the leader asked, "Lawyer B, you like the idea of taking prospective clients for lunch, but do you have any grave concerns about A's not taking prospective clients to lunch?" And Lawyer B said, "No."

They realized in that moment, of course, that it did not matter whether they had different styles and different approaches as long as they were both effective in their own ways.

In conducting meetings, you may frequently need to protect individuals who are respectfully disagreeing with one another by reminding them that different approaches for different people are quite acceptable.

Identifying the Topic and Creating Options

We all know people who seem to be more negative and critical than others. Someone in a meeting (Lawyer C) will put forward an idea, such as, "We should have a practice-group brochure or newsletter, some piece of material that we can give to clients and prospective clients." The negative person (Lawyer D) will immediately suggest that this is a terrible idea, exclaiming, "I'm absolutely opposed to that. It's going to be too expensive. It's going to be too time-consuming. I think it's an inappropriate thing for us to do."

Here you have the recipe for a nice divisive debate that will consume all of the time you had budgeted for the rest of the meeting and take you absolutely nowhere—except to leave the members of the group feeling as though they are unable get along and cannot accomplish anything together.

One facilitation method that is highly effective in situations such as this is for the leader to rise above the issue to a higher level of abstraction. In our illustration, the leader may say to Lawyer D, "You think that this is a silly, ridiculous, stupid, inappropriate, expensive idea. Well then, how do you think we might communicate with prospective clients more effectively?" At this point, Lawyer D may suddenly become highly constructive and very valuable to the group. He or she might say, "Well, I think we can use our Web site more effectively. I think we can use e-mail more successfully. I think there are a lot of tools we have that would be far less expensive and would yield us the same results."

In this scenario, Lawyer C was actually using the newsletter or brochure merely as an example of a bigger idea—a way of communicating with clients. Lawyer D is not at odds with the idea, only with the way of executing it.

As leader, you will find it useful to keep an eye on the issues that are at the heart of the discussion so you can help the group rise above them. You need to determine what concept or notion is really on the table for consideration, and how you can get the people in your group to contribute constructively to creating a list of alternative ways to accomplish that objective.

But now suppose that Lawyers C and D dig in their heels and become quite polarized. Lawyer C says, "I insist that a newsletter or brochure is the most cost-effective, efficient way to deal with the clients I have in mind," and Lawyer D says, "I think it's wrong that we should use our limited budget in that manner." If you cannot get them to agree at a higher level of abstraction on the notion, then at the very least you, as the meeting leader, may be able to generate some options.

On the flip chart in front of the group, you might write "brochures," and "newsletters." You might add "e-mail" and "Web site enhancement" to the list, and then say to the group, "What other avenues could we employ to accomplish this communications objective?" Your goal at this point is to get people to contribute other alternative ideas. In many cases the group will be able to create a prolific-enough list of options that they will find something that is of wide acceptance to the group.

Even if this does not happen, at least it gives you the opportunity to canvass the group. You can ask them to go down the list you have created and, with a show of hands, to indicate the extent of the support for the various ideas. As a side benefit, if the show of hands is nine to one in favor of the brochure, then the comments of the person who is vociferously opposed will immediately take on less significance.

Identifying the Roots of Polarization

As a leader you will frequently find people polarizing themselves within your group meetings. You are going to find people wanting to debate—in fact, some of them enjoy it simply for the sport.

Our training in the law means that sometimes when we want to know more about a subject we will take an opposing view just to stimulate the person proposing the idea, encouraging them to go deeper or give us stronger reasons to accept their point of view. Judges do this all the time—lawyers often come back from court situations reporting that the judge was terrible, only to find out later that the judge has decided in their favor. The judge was simply asking the lawyer to dig deeper to give the judge better reasons for his or her judgment, to make appeal less likely.

Some lawyers carry the same approach into meetings, and take a posture or an approach to stimulate the thinking of others. If you have someone in your group who seems to be opposed to something, you do not need to assume that they are actually opposed. In situations like that, carefully canvass group members for their views, and you may be surprised to learn that the person you think is opposed to an idea is not opposed to it at all. You owe it to yourself and the group to canvass for that reason.

Working with Group Dynamics

One other best practice will help you to be a more effective leader in meetings—and that is to lead from the principle that the weight of the meeting should not be on your shoulders alone. Less-experienced leaders sometimes think that it is their responsibility to make sure the meeting runs completely smoothly and ends up with wonderful results. If someone disagrees with something that is fundamentally important to the group, that leader will make the huge mistake of thinking that it is up to him or her to straighten out that group member.

Such an assumption nearly always leads to trouble. Remember how in law school, when a professor was very harsh with one individual student, a few other students would come to the assistance of the one who was drowning? The same thing will occur in your group meetings. You take on a member of your group and several other people will—for sport, if for no other reason—defend that individual and attack you. This is simply part of basic group dynamics. No matter how gifted and powerful you are, you cannot take on your entire group if they all come to get you with their swords unsheathed.

Effective leaders throw situations like this back to the group. Perhaps an individual challenges something which is very basic to the direction in which the group is going—he or she may say, for example, "I think it's inappropriate to open a branch office in [so-and-so]," or "I do not think we should move forward with this plan for attracting clients." It does not matter what the issue is—the point is that someone is vehemently opposed.

Instead of reacting, instead of debating, effective leaders turn to the group and say, "Are there any other thoughts on that?"

Almost without fail, someone in the rest of the group will balance the argument. If someone senior and powerful has made the argument, somebody else senior and powerful—or some unrestrained young Turk—will challenge that individual. This phenomenon is so reliable that it is almost amazing to watch. Like air filling a vacuum in physics, someone will come along to balance the argument.

At this point, you as a leader are in a far better position to handle the situation, because now you have people expressing different views about a matter. You can now say, "Well, let me just see if I understand. A is expressing a concern about such-and-so. B is telling us that she strongly believes such-and-such. Is there a way we can reconcile those points of view? Is there a way that we can satisfy both those concerns and still move forward as a group?"

It can be a grave mistake to assume that the weight of the meeting is on your shoulders alone; if you do believe this, you will fail. The best leaders know how to put contentious issues back to the group members, and allow the group to sort them out, so that that leader can maintain the role of leader.

Chapter 28

Defining and Fostering Creative Thinking

When I ask the managing partners of good law firms, "Do you see creativity in your firm? Do you see situations where innovation is occurring?" the answer is always an unqualified "yes." Typically I hear such comments as, "We have professionals who are synergistic, and who combine disciplines to get results that otherwise wouldn't have been available," or "Our professionals have highly creative and extraordinary ideas for solving problems," or at least, "I think from time to time we do a wonderful job at that."

Well, in most cases, I beg to differ. Based on what I have observed about the way most firms actually operate, the propensity to be innovative or creative is pretty well drummed out of people right at the outset.

Let us examine how this happens. Imagine that some junior person has an idea—perhaps that the firm could employ a bit of technology to do this or that part of its work more effectively. The junior person proposes his idea to someone senior, and the senior person's typical reaction is, "Is there any other law firm doing that?" If not, forget it. And if some other law firm *is* doing that, the law firm is never good enough to emulate.

The junior person gets the message in short order that coming up with creative or innovative ideas is not the way to impress the power people in the firm. What impresses them is really good billable hours, really good billings, and the occasional client attraction.

Well, so what?

The "so what" is that in a highly competitive world, where things are changing at the speed of light, where e-commerce is much more important than many traditional areas of practice, we need our people to be versatile. We need them to be flexible. We need them to be resilient. More often today than ever before, people will start the practice of law in one area and finish it in another. Even just one generation ago, the majority of people spent their entire practicing lifetime in one area of specialty. So we need to inject into our firms the ability to innovate, the ability to be creative, so that we will be in a better position to adapt to the rapid changes that are certain to continue be a fact of life in future.

Lateral Thinking

One individual who is very much worth reading on the subject of creativity is Edward de Bono—probably the greatest authority alive today on subjects related to thinking and the range of thinking methodologies. Single-handedly he has made what is likely the greatest contribution not only to the way professionals and business leaders think, but also to the ways in which our children are educated.

De Bono talks about a process he calls "lateral thinking," and explains the difference between that and our normal thinking processes, which are usually quite linear. In linear thinking, when we are faced with a problem, we tend to revert to the pattern we used to solve the last problem.

He asks us to imagine our brains as though they were bowls of Jell-O®, and to think of solving problems as pouring some boiling water onto that Jell-O from a teaspoon. When this happens time and time again, the boiling water begins to make crevices through the gelatin. As we pour more and more water on the bowl of Jell-O, the water tends to follow the same paths because the crevices get deeper and deeper. De Bono describes lateral thinking as a way of starting a new place on that bowl of Jell-O, to follow a path we have not followed before.

A practical application of lateral thinking to problem solving in a law-practice setting might involve the question of how to attract more clients from the retail industry. If we were to convene a traditional meeting and follow a traditional pattern of linear thinking on the subject, we would probably come up with a list very quickly that would include such ideas as creating some brochures or sending out a newsletter, doing an advertisement, targeting certain individuals in the industry with whom we could meet, and so on. That would be a pretty predictable pattern.

De Bono suggests that in order to get out of our traditional ruts, we apply lateral thinking to the problem by taking a word at random (nouns work best)—chosen perhaps by stabbing a finger at an open dictionary page—and that we do four things with that word in relation to our problem. First, we define it. Secondly, we describe its function. Thirdly, we "free associate" with it, and finally, we create puns with it, if possible. While we are doing those four things, he suggests that we keep our problem in mind and see whether any of the areas we cover in relation to the word might suggest solutions or ideas that might be useful to us.

Let us say that the word that comes up in our sample situation is "table." First we define table—perhaps as "something that supports something else."

Okay. Now we look at the word "supports" and apply it to our situation. How can we be more supportive of the people in the industry we are trying to attract? Well, maybe we could provide them with better information. Maybe we could offer a seminar for them. Maybe we could contribute money to the industry association or take a booth at their annual meeting.

In expanding our definition of what a table is, we might decide that it is "flat" or "even." This description might suggest to us that we need a smoother approach to attracting clients in the area under discussion. Or maybe we should flatten out our efforts so that we are not doing the majority of our activity in February and then none in April. Some of these ideas may seem to be a stretch, but that is part of the intention of the exercise—it stretches our thinking processes.

Now we move on to de Bono's second step by looking at the function of a table. It may be a conference table. It may bring people together. Applying lateral thinking to our original problem, we now ask ourselves, how can we bring appropriate people together from the industry in a way that might be useful to them? Perhaps we could include people from other industries who would be of interest to our target industry.

In this manner, the group proceeds through the four exercises with the randomly selected word, applying each one to its problem.

Again and again I have seen how—by following de Bono's suggestions regarding lateral thinking—groups can add to their list of options some additional and diverse items that might never have been there otherwise. Is it fun? Yes, it can be a bit of fun. More importantly, is it productive? Absolutely. A lateral-thinking initiative is hugely productive because it may take us to an idea or a tactic which has some significant competitive advantage, and one which our competitors would not have thought of because they tend to approach these things in a far more linear, traditional manner.

I assure you that if you try this methodology, the solutions and ideas you come up with will be far more creative, far more refreshing than the ones on your linear list. Find an excuse to try this on your own, using your journal. You will impress yourself with your results.

Encouraging Creativity

I have seen a number of different firms and groups within firms do some amazing things to foster creativity. For example—believe it or not—one practice group, in its search for a basis for interacting with one another in completely different ways, settled on the idea of creating a painting together. They went out and bought paints and brushes and canvas and together they made a painting. By doing so, they gave themselves the opportunity to approach each other in a way that they had not approached each other before, and to do something that had nothing to do with their traditional practice area to see if that activity might provide a new element that would stimulate greater creativity.

Some organizations actually make tools for creativity available on a more enduring basis. In some offices, for example, there are white boards placed on the walls here and there in the hallways between offices, so that if two people are walking down the hall or talking in the hallway and they have an idea, they can grab a marker pen and begin.

It doesn't matter which tools you use, the important thing is to foster a work environment that fundamentally supports and perhaps even visibly encourages the use of creativity in problem-solving situations. An associated challenge is to neutralize the propensities and procedures that conspire to discourage creativity.

Chapter 29

Meetings That Foster Creative Thinking

There are some lawyers in some firms who think that they are simply no good at being creative, and should not be expected to participate in creative endeavors. They think that they should be left alone with their critical and analytical abilities to create a quality legal work product. This is a myth that we should shatter. The most analytical and critical minds can be highly creative if they allow themselves to be. Becoming more creative in our thought patterns simply requires that we break existing patterns—including the traditional analytical and critical approach.

It is important to examine how creativity works. Creativity is not necessarily a phenomenon whereby one person sits silently in a room and decides that $E = MC^2$ or writes a symphony. Creative thinking does not need to be a solitary endeavor. Most people find it much easier to be creative in a diverse group where people are able to bounce ideas off one another, where people are allowed to go off on tangents, where people feel free to say silly things and explore unusual ideas. As we have previously mentioned, sometimes something that initially sounds unusual or silly starts to make sense when someone else adds another dimension to it.

The rules for brainstorming that we discussed in previous chapters are also useful to creative thinking in group settings. The most important rule is that people are not allowed to value-judge ideas before they are thoroughly examined. Again, in a typical meeting with lawyers, as soon as an idea is expressed someone expresses a counterview—"Let me tell you why that won't work," or "Let me tell you what I worry about when you talk about doing that," or "Let me tell you about the exceptional costs that might incur for us," or "Let me tell you who that might offend." In order to break that pattern, we need to set a ground rule: Until we have completely explored what our options are, we will not value-judge any of them. We will simply, creatively build an ideas list.

To foster creativity within your group, you need to obtain group agreement in advance that:

1) going off on tangents is encouraged;
2) during the course of the discussion no one will be allowed to dump on anyone else's ideas; and
3) a great deal of flexibility and free-flowing thought will be the order of the day.

Out of that kind of process, you will find that some worthwhile ideas, thoughts, and plans arise that would otherwise never have been discovered.

The Value of New Surroundings

In order to successfully build ideas, you may also need to change environments. Settings can constrain us. If you doubt this, just go back to the school where you studied law, and walk into the room where you wrote your most significant exam. How do you feel in that environment? Do you feel your stomach tensing up? Similarly, how do you feel in your office when you look at your "mental block" files over on the credenza?

Familiar walls can limit the freedom people feel to allow themselves to be creative. For this reason, many firms find it productive to get away from the office environment for some of their deliberations—they may go to a retreat setting, for example.

I have seen groups work very well in highly unusual environments. I once served on a national committee of the Canadian Bar Association (CBA) that was comprised primarily of very senior, very traditional lawyers. It was our task to figure out how to develop a more effective system of disseminating worthwhile papers that had been drafted by learned people in various areas of the law among lawyers throughout Canada.

The committee wanted to make a deliberate effort not to be encumbered by traditional thinking. We wanted to be quite creative. So we decided we would have our meeting in a hot tub. We had our director sit on the edge of the hot tub with a pad of paper on a clipboard to take notes, and away we went, thinking about what ideas we might develop.

As we were working, a man we did not know who simply happened to be staying in the same hotel and happened to be in the same hot tub, observed our group of lawyers behaving in this admittedly abnormal-for-lawyers fashion. After he had listened to our discussion for awhile, he said, "Do you mind if I say something?" And we said, "No," and he said, "If you don't mind my saying it, you lawyers have a pretty bad reputation. You have a pretty bad public image."

Well, this man was not telling us anything we had not heard before, but we did accept what he had said. We thanked him and we said, "You're quite right." And then one of our group asked him, "Have you any ideas on what we might do to improve our image?" At that point, we got into an interesting discussion. (An amusing aside: We asked this man what he did for a living, and when he said he was a chiropractor, it occurred to me that it may have been the case of people who live in glass houses throwing stones.)

As a result of what took place, that silly-sounding meeting in a hot tub not only helped us to develop a methodology for disseminating those papers—a system that turned out to be highly successful and very profitable for the CBA—it also provided a side consequence, an unintended benefit. The committee decided that, from that moment forward, a member of some other industry or profession would always be appointed to our committee, and would deliberate with us.

In other words, because of the diverse and different thinking that the chiropractor brought to our meeting, the lawyers on that committee decided that we should never again proceed without the benefit of an outside viewpoint. They felt that a different point of view would always be valuable—irrespective of exactly where it came from.

Can you apply a similar notion to your situation? Can you include in your deliberations someone who is not a lawyer—a person who might have a different perspective on your situation? Some groups are quite narrow-minded. They think, "How could anyone who is not a lawyer possibly add any value to our deliberations?" I would suggest that such a viewpoint be carefully reconsidered. Many firms benefit considerably from including support professionals who are not lawyers in their meetings—marketing or training professionals, for example. Some actually include such individuals *because* they do not come from a traditional perspective; they appreciate the nontraditional input.

Six Hats

One further concept of Edward de Bono is also directly relevant to increasing the potential for success in law firms and practice groups. It is set out in one of de Bono's best-known books, *Six Thinking Hats*.

You might be asking yourself what the significance of six hats might be to the practice of law, or more specifically to the development of your practice. Well, in this context, the "six hats" exercise addresses our propensities as lawyers to adhere to certain thought patterns by requiring us to think in different ways.

The six hats are white, purple, yellow, red, green, and blue.

- The person wearing the white hat thinks about facts and details, asking such questions as, "Do we have enough information?" "Is there enough specificity?"
- The person in the purple hat considers the negative aspects of the topic (this would be the natural default thinking mode for many of us in the profession, so some lucky person gets to be purple and do this deliberately).
- The wearer of the yellow hat finds and focuses on the positive aspects of the topic under discussion (this task can be a little more challenging for many practitioners of the law).
- The person in the red hat looks at the topic from the point of view of emotions or feelings, positive or negative—raising such questions, for example, as "How would we feel as a group if we went ahead with this idea?" or "Might such an approach not irritate [Client A] at the expense of [Client B]?" This is often an interesting challenge for the designated "red" spokesperson as it requires a very different perspective from the one we normally use to examine problems.
- The wearer of the green hat is required to contribute imaginative or lateral thinking—perhaps using techniques like the ones described in the previous chapter—to come up with something relating to the topic that is far more innovative and creative than has been raised before.
- The wearer of the blue hat focuses on reflection, or meta-cognition. Meta-cognition consists of three basic elements: 1) *Developing* a plan of action; 2) *Maintaining/monitoring* the plan; 3) *Evaluating* the plan. So in a sense, the blue hat considers how the idea might receive the "breath of life."

Let us imagine again that we have a practice or industry group that is looking at a particular business development objective, such as attracting more quality clients in a chosen area. Perhaps we have created a plan and we want to review and examine it more carefully. Now, imagine the power of the six people you brought together, six smart people—maybe you chose a few of them at random to make this a little more fun and a little less personal.

At this point, I have seen sophisticated professional groups actually assemble hats of those different colors and hand them out to members of their teams. At the very least you need to hand out pieces of paper with one of the colors written on each one, and ask each individual to please take on a role consistent with that color as the matter is discussed.

Think of the advantages.

Number one, people are not as likely to be criticized for their points of view because it is clear that they are carrying out a function that they were asked to carry out. The negative person, for example, will not be criticized for being overly negative—it is his or her job to do that. Whatever the result or outcome in a particular situation, the topic is likely to receive a far more diverse assessment than would otherwise have occurred. At the end of the six-hat exercise, the group can explore what it has learned, and what areas it wants to pursue as a result of its deliberations from these various perspectives.

The purpose of the exercises described in this chapter and the previous one is to help you and your firm look at innovation, look at creativity, and think about getting away from traditional linear thought processes. It is intended to help you—when appropriate—to see ways to be far more creative, far more innovative, and far more imaginative than is normally the case. I have explained a couple of tools that Edward de Bono has invented, and presented some methodologies that I have seen work effectively in different firms, but the challenge is really yours.

What do you think would work in your environment? What do you think you might import into your situation that might get your people to be more creative, that might get *you* to be more creative and imaginative—giving you choices you would not otherwise have had?

Thinking about how you might foster more creativity within your firm is a worthwhile endeavor. It will contribute not only to your competitive advantage, but also to your sense of satisfaction.

Chapter 30

Dealing with Difficult People

I have worked closely with many leaders in firms around the world—including managing partners, leaders of industry, practice and client groups, leaders of production teams, and others. A common denominator among these individuals is their concern about working with someone in their group who is extremely difficult.

These leaders are not usually complaining about people who cause isolated incidents. They are talking about dysfunctional human beings who are absolutely terrible when it comes to working in groups. We have acknowledged the ferocious independence of lawyers in general, but these people take that independence to an absolute extreme. They often occupy a corner office. They often bill a lot of money—which, by the way, is one of the reasons why they are allowed to stay. But they are lone rangers.

Leaders say, "How am I supposed to lead a group that contains someone like [X]? They hoard work. They are not collaborative. Sometimes their interpersonal relationships within the firm, among support staff and junior fee-earners, for example, are so horrible that it is demoralizing. They don't mentor or supervise anyone, even though we wish they would. They don't participate in the internal skill programs. They are just very, very difficult."

In some of the worst cases, these people actually sabotage the operation of the group. They quietly wait without expressing their views while decisions are made, and then they act completely inconsistently with those decisions. Their approach is consistently "counter-group" or "counter-team."

Direct Communication

Some leaders have found that a very effective course of action for situations involving people like this is to communicate directly with the difficult individual. This communication may occur prior to a weekend meeting of the firm or of the group, or perhaps before a routine meeting. In any event the leader takes the time and finds the patience to chat with the difficult individual, asking whether they have any concerns about any of the issues or topics or situations that may be dealt with at the meeting.

Sometimes the difficult person will have a lot of concerns indeed. For example, they may worry that by virtue of some of the decisions the group might take, they might lose some of their autonomy—their control over their own practice. "After all," they may wonder, "if we are supposed to work collaboratively, then does that mean I can't do things my own way any more?" The individual may have concerns of this nature, and other concerns as well.

There is absolutely nothing wrong with a leader's making the effort to understand the concerns of an individual in the group—even if that individual happens to be difficult, or even obnoxious. Having listened to that person's concerns, and understood them, the effective leader is now in a position to offer some assurances. The leader says something like, "Well, you are extremely well regarded for the practice you have in the [such-and-so] area, and I think the last thing the group wants to do is get in your way or hamper your style. Why don't I undertake that I will do my best to ensure that the group does not take any unnecessary or gratuitous steps that might unduly interfere with the way you like to do things. And, indeed, if something like that occurs, then by all means let's talk about it. Let us see if we can work it out in a way that will be satisfactory to you."

Exacting a Promise

The leader has now listened to the individual, and gained a little bit of that person's trust, and presented the person with some assurances. Now they are in a position to ask for something in return. At this point, many good leaders will talk candidly with the individual about what is expected of them when it comes to the meeting. The leader may ask, for example, that the individual pause and consider the effect and the force of their views when they express them in the meeting.

The leader may couch his or her expectations in words like this: "You may not realize the persuasive power you have simply because of your seniority or by virtue of the practice you conduct. When you state a view or an opinion, it may have more force than if someone newer or more junior were to express the same opinion. Therefore I want to ask that you be careful not to express negative views or concerns in a way that might take the wind out of the sails of some of our junior people." If the person is senior, the leader might add, "Think back to when you were new. Think back to when a comment from a senior partner in the firm had a huge influence over you. Be guided by that as you think about what you say in the meeting."

In my experience, even powerful and difficult people will listen to that statement. Indeed, it will ring true for them. Some senior, powerful members of the firm simply do not remember or focus on the fact that especially for brand-new people or junior people, what they say has tremendous weight, tremendous influence. Sometimes they may not realize that their concern or negativity about some issue can have a tremendous impact on the group. Reminding them of that may in itself be sufficient to get them to moderate their behavior.

In some situations it is fair to go even further, and to say, "In exchange for the assurances I have given you, I'd like to ask that you refrain, if possible, from expressing negative views about where we're going as a group, because I think that may demoralize some of our junior people. I need their vigor, I need their best efforts, I need their peak performance, and candidly, I don't want anything to happen at the meeting that is going to detract from that. Is that fair?"

Again, many leaders report that even the most difficult powerful and senior people can understand that kind of request, and will in many cases be quite accommodating.

Worst-Case Scenarios

You may feel that I am expressing some rather optimistic views here. You may be thinking, "You just do not understand how difficult X is in our firm."

Indeed, there may be situations where the difficult people in your firm do not even show up at meetings—where there is nothing you can do to even get them to a meeting. There may also be situations extreme enough when they do participate that you want to exclude them from your meetings.

I appreciate the seriousness of your dilemma here. In conducting group sessions, the absence of one of the most senior, powerful members of the group may seem rather negative. At the same time, it may be more productive to let the people who want to achieve something together get on with it—without that individual—than to simply have them there for the sake of appearances. (Of course, if you do exclude someone, it is politic to tell them in advance, and to explain why you are doing it.)

A Note to Meeting Participants

Much of the content in this chapter is directed to the leader who runs a group or organizes a group. You may be in a group where there is a very difficult person with whom you have to contend, where you are not in a leadership role, but are, in effect, a peer. In such cases, think through the steps outlined here for the leader, and consider following them on your own. There is nothing to prevent you from one-on-one interaction with the difficult individual, nothing to prevent you from asking about his or her concerns and listening to them, and nothing to prevent you from giving assurances in terms of your working together. You might well be able to adapt these methods to suit the group's objectives.

Dealing with Underachievers

In working with the support staffs of many good firms, I have observed that if you want to annoy, frustrate, and demoralize a secretary, you should place an incompetent secretary next to the first one, then tolerate that second secretary's incompetent behavior—in other words, do not do anything about it.

We all hate being forced to work with people who are not accomplishing anything. Whether you are a sole practitioner leading your support team or whether you are dealing with an entire practice area in a mega-firm, you need to ask yourself whether you are tolerating people within your group who are demoralizing others. If you are, you need to reflect on whether it is worth it to do that.

In many cases, these nonproductive individuals will bill enough or attract enough clientele or, in the case of support staff, will simply have been around long enough or be capable of causing you enough concern about doing something about the situation that it is easier to leave it alone—to turn a blind eye to it. However, consider it this way: you may have some poison in your midst, and this poison can thwart the kind of performance you want from the other people with whom you work. Maybe failing to do anything about this kind of situation is costing you more than you think.

If you are dealing with problem performance of someone you supervise or lead, then you will want to do everything you reasonably can to resolve the situation before doing anything drastic. Best practices in dealing with such circumstances may include the following steps:

1) Communicate with the person who is underachieving. As you do so, remember to separate the person from the behavior. The discussion is not about them; it is some component of their performance that is causing a concern.

2) Do not enter the discussion with your mind made up regarding conclusions and remedies. This is somewhat akin to the best practices in dealing with clients. Go into your meeting ready to express your concerns, and ready to listen. Say, "I understand that there may be a problem related to [such-and-so]. What is your take on that? Is this correct in your view? Have you any thoughts? What is your perspective on this?" Listen to what you hear next. Some people are defensive, and some will simply avoid confronting the problem. You may have to persist, but you do need to begin by allowing that person to express his or her point of view, and by listening to it and understanding it.

3) Look with that person for a joint solution to the problem. Say, "How might we work through this in a way that is acceptable to you? In other words, can I help you resolve this problem? Is there anything I can do that would assist you in getting past this?" You may need to show leadership by offering solutions that would be helpful to that individual, but if possible you want to encourage that person to offer potential solutions first. As in the case of unhappy clients, if you can live with one of the other person's solutions, you are likely to have a far more effective outcome than if the solution is imposed by you.

4) Finally—and this is not an easy step—you need to set a timetable by which jointly and together you will measure whether the problem is being resolved.

After taking these steps, if the problem is resolved, then you are a hero. If the problem is not resolved, then you have a very unpleasant task ahead of you.

In some parts of the world, dismissing someone—even from a working group—is almost unheard of, almost impossible. In other parts of the world it is less so. But no matter where you are located, unless you come to grips with these kinds of situations, you are doing a disservice to yourself and to the people with whom you work. There are too many uncomfortable situations where people simply fail to take necessary action.

My encouragement to you in this difficult task is as follows: if you do not do it for yourself, do it for the people with whom you work. They will be grateful to you.

Part V

The Business Side of Law

Chapter 31

Being More Entrepreneurial

A number of years ago, I made a transition from working as an active, practicing lawyer and law-firm managing partner, to become a co-founder of a consultancy. There are many similarities between practicing law and serving as a consultant to the legal profession. In fact, quite a number of the methodologies and approaches which serve me well in my current work, and which I endeavor to share with others, were ones I acquired during my service to my law firm and our clients.

There is, however, one distinction that I would like to bring to your attention that I learned by chance. It is the difference between being a "lawyer" and being an "entrepreneur," and it relates to our approach to new situations and challenges.

By training, lawyers learn to *look back* to find out what worked before, so that we can offer predictability to our clients. What do we do when we draft a document, for example? We look for clauses that have been tested by a court. Why? Because we want to have a predictable outcome should they be tested again. That is simply good lawyering; in fact, not to proceed in this fashion would probably be negligent.

That approach, however, tends to give most of us a backward-looking, and extremely conservative, mind-set. We do not want to do anything unless it has already been done.

I tease members of law firms that when they are looking at a methodology or something that might serve them into the future, the first question someone senior often asks is, "Does any other law firm do this?"—and usually that question is the kiss of death to the proposal.

Think of the possible responses. On one hand, it might be, "No, I don't think any other law firm is doing this," to which the senior person is likely to reply, "Well, we're certainly not going to be the first."

On the other hand, the answer could be, "Yes, indeed. There is a law firm already doing this."

"Oh yeah?" they will say. "Which one?"

"Well, the law firm of [ABC] is doing this."

"Right," we will hear at that point. "The day we do something in this great firm that they're doing over at [ABC] will be my last day as a partner here."

In short, our approach is typically extremely conservative and careful and is a splendid perspective for lawyering. I do not encourage you to lose it, and I do not intend to lose it either, for when we practice law we need to bring it to the table. However, it does us a great disservice when we are building businesses.

The Entrepreneurial Mind-set

Entrepreneurs think about possibilities. Entrepreneurs want to be creative. They want to be innovative. They do not take silly risks or unnecessary risks, but what they do is to consistently look for better and better ways of doing things. Why? Because they know that in a competitive world, they need an advantage. They know they need to be the first ones with a methodology that will give the client or customer better value. They need to be the first ones to deliver a service in a way that is superior to the way any other person has ever delivered it.

How much of an entrepreneur are you in the practice of law?

What innovations have you been responsible for?

What methodologies have you changed?

What improvements have you made to the way in which your work is done?

What needs have you anticipated of your clients that go beyond the traditional needs of clients in your practice areas, or in the industries you serve?

If you are answering these questions with words like, "Hmmm. Not very many of those," or "Not much of that," you may be guilty—as most of us have been—of not being entrepreneurial at all in the practice of law.

"So what?" you might reply. "Why should I be entrepreneurial? What's wrong with simply being a good lawyer?"

There is nothing much wrong with just being a good lawyer if you are not interested in going anywhere. (This statement is not meant to be disrespectful, merely realistic.) Let me put it this way: law firms are no longer giving anybody tenure.

Years ago, if you were a partner in a good firm, you had it made. Nobody was ever going to ask you to leave unless you did something really scandalous. Today law firms are continuously measuring the performance of every human being who works there. In fact, firms today are measuring performance with greater and greater sophistication, in ways they never did before—not only in terms of billings and revenues, but in terms of profitability of matters, profitability by work area, profitability by client, profitability by discipline or industry group, and so on. The sophistication of evaluation systems is enhanced so much that all of us have become more vulnerable to being measured in terms of our real value to a firm.

The Need for an Entrepreneurial Approach to the Practice of Law

Some of the most sophisticated clients in the world—and in this regard you have probably read about great companies like DuPont—are using fewer and fewer law firms, while at the same time demanding of those firms greater and greater dedication to technology, knowledge sharing, and so on. In other words, clients are driving the demand for firms to be better and better and better.

Where does this leave you?

Well, you can wait until a significant client insists on a better methodology or threatens to fire you in favor of someone else, or you can wait until you wake up one morning and the client is simply gone, and discover later that they left for another firm where they could get more value or a better process or better service . . . or whatever.

Or you can be a pioneer.

You can be a pioneer with your clients in the industries you serve by finding out what their future needs look like. You can ask yourself such questions as, "How can I assemble imaginative people who can incrementally help us become more and more valuable to this client and others in their industry?"

Lawyers with that attitude—lawyers who consistently work to improve themselves and to give greater value to their clients—end up as long-term winners. In this day and age, it is to their firms that the better clients gravitate.

To breathe life into this idea for yourself, take a moment and note in your journal at least one small action you can take in the next few days that will start you on your journey to being more entrepreneurial. Note your progress and add further steps as appropriate. By doing this, you will make more headway than you might have thought you would, and you will put yourself far ahead of those who turn the page without putting pen to paper.

Chapter 32

A Reason for Business Development

Some years ago, I was invited to write a book for Butterworths on the subject of practice development, ultimately titled *Practice Development: Creating the Marketing Mindset*. That book forced me to look very carefully at a number of the individual components involved in developing a practice. This chapter of the book draws together the fundamental issues that I touched upon back then, adding many additional ideas that I have observed since as best practices, in working with the best professional firms in the world.

Planning to Achieve Your Goals

If you were to ask a lawyer at random, "What kind of work will you be doing next week or next month?" the answer will typically be, "I don't know yet."

If you then ask, "Okay. So you don't know. How will you find out?" the answer is likely to be, "Well, it depends what letter comes in. It depends what phone calls I receive. Basically, I will do what clients and prospective clients ask me to do."

In the short term, that is pretty much how law practices are run. We are busy. We are engaged day-to-day with our existing cases, and when people ask us to do other things we do them.

Short term, that probably is a fine way to manage a legal practice, but as a long-term approach it is absolutely wrong. For the long term, we need to look to the plan we created for ourselves back in Chapters 1 and 2, and look to the kind of work we want to do and the kind of clients for whom we want to do that work. Then we need to deploy some of our time to steering our practice in the direction we want it to go. In the context of The Successful Lawyer program, "business development" is all about helping you find a more fulfilling, more exciting practice.

In the planning process you looked at the kinds of clients you enjoy serving. You also thought about the kinds of work—the kinds of legal matters—you enjoy doing the most. You completed an exercise in which you examined a matter that you had really enjoyed working on, and then reflected on what the nature of that matter was and what you brought to it that really made it fulfilling for you. That was the beginning step in discovering how you would want to shape your practice.

Refresh your memory by glancing back at those notes right now—it will make the following chapters more meaningful to you as we explore how to make your dreams a reality.

Chapter 33

Moving Toward Emerging Areas

It is instructive to examine closely how legal services move from the "emerging" stage, when they are specialties, through the "growing" and then "mature" stages, and finally into the "declining" stage, when they become commodities.

In the *emerging* stage, a legal service is fairly new. Not very many clients know they might need it, and not many lawyers know how to provide it. In the early part of the twenty-first century, emerging areas include biomedical law, genetic law, the law that influences intellectual property rights to genetically altered things, and related areas: this is a reasonably new field of law. Not very many lawyers know all that much about it, and not that many clients know how they might utilize services in this field. Still, it is an area that is definitely emerging.

At the emerging stage of a legal service, the hourly rates are high. The leverage is low because not much can be passed on to juniors in that area, but it is very rewarding for people who are involved in this stage of the practice.

An example today of an area in the *growing* stage might be environmental law. Although in some parts of the world environmental law is still fairly new, in most places this field has been growing for some considerable period of time. "Growing" areas tend to be areas where most good law firms do some of that kind of work and have some people with expertise in the field, and many clients understand its relevance and importance and even think from time to time that they might need to employ services in that area. However, the field is still short of the next stage, which is the mature stage.

The *mature* stage is that stage when a legal service has been around long enough that every good law firm is practicing in that area, and almost every appropriate client knows about the service. In fact, the work is often beginning to move in-house. In-house counsel are beginning to realize that they can create that legal work product at a lower cost by having their own in-house lawyers do it than by employing private firms outside. A good example of this in current practice might include work with routine banking documents such as debentures or mortgages.

Finally we reach the *declining* stage. At this point, the work begins to fall off the radar screen. In fact, it begins to leave the profession. Such areas today include residential real-estate deals and uncontested divorces. In some parts of the world, firms that are not law firms are doing residential real-estate transactions, for example. As for uncontested divorces, as this book was being written, experiments were being conducted that actually utilized computers and the equivalent of automated teller machines to help people resolve their property settlements in simple matrimonial disputes.

Lawyers who practice in "declining" fields of law experience tremendous downward fee pressure. The public perceives that the work is a commodity that is available from a number of different sources, and at that point service, quality, and price become the most important issues.

Applying the Specialty/Commodity Continuum to Your Practice

The relevance to you of an analysis of the specialty/commodity continuum is, of course, that as you plan your future, as you plan how you want to steer your practice, not only do you want to avoid the "declining" end of the curve, you want to strive continually to move closer to the "emerging" end.

Decisions about fields of law on which to focus in this regard are complicated by the fact that when you go inside a particular practice area, you discover that each also contains its own curve. In the field of employment law, for example, you might ask yourself such questions as:

- What aspects are becoming mature or even heading towards decline?
- What is perceived as routine? What aspects are going in-house?

- What are the new areas? What are the challenging areas?
- What new legislation or new kinds of risk management or litigation are emerging?

Similar questions can productively be asked in other areas of law. In other words, the "emerging–growing–maturing–declining" analysis can be done either in a macro sense—across different practice areas—or in a micro sense: within a particular practice area.

The issue here is the same. Your job in terms of managing your future is to constantly ask yourself, "What is new in this area? What future needs for clients arising from this particular practice area are just around the corner?"

Focus your thoughts by writing in your journal—explore how you can make the ideas in this chapter part of the way you practice law.

Among other reasons, conducting an analysis of this kind is extremely important because it relates to *your* value. The more effectively you move toward the emerging area of either your existing practice area or other practice areas that appeal to you, the more valuable you will be in the future to your existing and prospective clients.

The more valuable you are, the higher your rates will be. The higher your rates are, the more successful you will be financially. Furthermore, that success will come to you with a smaller investment of time.

Chapter 34

Industry Group Tactics

At this point in the history of legal practice and the evolution of the way clients view and purchase legal services, there is merit in close examination of the difference between organizing our practices by traditional substantive practice areas versus organizing by the industries to which our clients belong.

In the past, lawyers in the United Kingdom were described essentially as either "barristers" or "solicitors." In other cultures they were known as, for example, "business lawyers" or "litigation lawyers." As things became more sophisticated, different practice areas emerged, and today some large firms have dozens of practice areas—ranging from real property to environmental law to intellectual property through corporate and commercial law, and so forth. As there is a positive correlation between the number of practice areas in a firm and its profitability, it appears that it is helpful to become highly specialized.

Having said that, as we focus on business development it is important to keep in mind that practice areas are orientations imposed by firms and lawyers. They are not client orientations. An individual client—let's say it is an entrepreneur in a high-tech area—does not care whether a lawyer is an intellectual property lawyer or a corporate lawyer or a litigator or a business lawyer or whatever other label we might apply. What that client or prospective client cares about is "Do you understand my business? Have you dealt with businesses like mine before? Do you understand my issues? Can you not only do my legal work by solving my legal problems, but can you also even tell me the kinds of issues I ought to be concerned about, or the kinds of things I

167

am likely to encounter in the future that I ought to be worrying about?"

Your clients and prospective clients are looking for answers to these kinds of questions. This is not a personal opinion of mine: I am reporting to you the results of millions and millions and millions of dollars worth of research done by some of the largest professional service firms in the world. Over and over again, that research has revealed that clients do not select professionals based on their substantive areas of expertise, but rather on their industry orientations.

What does this mean in terms of legal practice? It means that by focusing on traditional areas of the law, we are not touching on the business-development aspect of our practice.

Let us imagine that we create a graph, labeling the vertical lines with the traditional practice areas. We identify those areas on which we now focus, and those on which we wish to focus. We compare our strengths in different areas and determine where we wish to enhance our skills and become better lawyers. The problem is that no matter how laudable it sounds, this exercise will—in and of itself—do nothing to enhance business.

To market your practice, you need to draw horizontal lines on that same graph, and to begin describing—one by one—the kinds of industries that you either currently serve or might wish to serve. These could include the retail industry, the automotive industry, the manufacturing sector, high-tech, bionics, robotics—you name it; whatever industry or industries make sense and are relevant. By identifying an industry or a few industries, you can begin to consider tactics that would make you effective at targeting and attracting work from that industry or those industries.

Specific Industry Tactics

One of the most neglected ways of becoming effective from an industry perspective is to learn something about the industry. I have been amazed to review research that disclosed that many lawyers do not read even *one* publication from the industry in which their largest client resides. Think about that for a moment. We are not talking about reading hundreds of publications in several industries to become very knowledgeable, we are talking about reading *one* publication in the industry of one's *largest* client.

What kind of potential competitive advantage might this suggest to you? Clearly, it suggests some focus, some study, on the industries you are interested in serving or currently serve. You can do this research yourself, or even have someone else help you with it. You can subscribe to one or two publications in the relevant industry—even if all you do is skim the publications, reading very selectively. This one step alone will give you a competitive advantage.

There is a book called *Influence: The Psychology of Persuasion* by Robert B. Cialdini which is relevant to business development for professionals and professional service firms. Some of the findings in *Influence* are counterintuitive—which is one of the reasons why I find the book so valuable. As lawyers, we tend to assimilate information and grasp concepts very quickly, and as a result we have fairly high levels of confidence in our own speculation. We think we can hypothesize how things work, and how one thing will relate to another. However, it is in those situations when we find that our intuition was dead wrong that we can often really learn something.

Let me give you an illustration.

Most people assume that if we want someone to be interested in our future and to help us with our future, the way to get them to do that is do some kindness for them first—offer them some help. Sort of a "you scratch my back and I'll scratch yours" approach. Well, apparently our assumption in that area is wrong. According to *Influence*, the best way to get people interested in our development and in our future is to ask *them* for help.

Think about this for a moment. Have you ever had a client ask for your thoughts on how they might market their business better? Has a child who had to write a term paper ever asked for your advice as to how the paper might be structured, or what subject they might choose? Have you noticed that once your assistance has been asked for, and you have offered it, you have an investment in the outcome? You become very concerned. "Well, how did it go?" you ask. "Did you get a high grade on that paper?" "Were your marketing efforts successful?" This is a natural human response.

How can you put this response to work for you?

One thing you might do is to bring together some clients, and perhaps some prospective clients as well, for the purpose of assisting you in developing your industry expertise. You may want to make the situation a little more win-win—so that, rather than simply for your benefit, you create a bit of a round table where people will share knowledge that will be of benefit to everyone assembled. However, a basic purpose is to give you an opportunity to ask the advice of people in the industry about where they think the industry is going, what they think the industry's needs will be in the future, and so on.

You will find that by assisting you, these individuals will become invested in *your* outcome. They will want to know how your initiative is going. They will ask, "Is your practice developing along the industry lines you had in mind?" By taking an approach like this, sometimes the prospective clients you have included in the meeting will even decide to convert themselves into existing clients.

Chapter 35

Targeting Tactics

Up to this point in our discussion of the business side of law, we have:

- looked at the specialty/commodity curve;
- seen how we can move toward more-specialized work that commands higher hourly rates and more profitability; and
- considered the fact that clients choose professionals based on industry orientation, rather than on traditional substantive practice-group orientation.

As a practitioner, you have:

- begun to think about the industries that you want to serve, and
- looked at some tactics for learning about those industries—and even at some of the psychological processes you might put to work for you, such as asking people to help you develop your industry knowledge and expertise.

The final building block for developing the kind of practice you want to have is to actually identify prospective clients that you would like to attract.

Many people make the mistake of never getting definite about this step. If an individual or company chooses them to do something, they are pleased to have been selected and they want to do the work for that client. Their business-development activities amount to a shotgun approach— "Let's throw some ads together," "Let's do a brochure," "Let's do some seminars," "Let's go to meetings," "Let's get out in the public," "Let's join this organization," "Let's join that organization"—the principle being, if you are out there and people see you out there, the work will come.

Some work *will* come that way, but it will be diverse in nature. The shotgun approach will not get you the practice you want to have. Certainly, if you think it is appropriate, you can do some of this kind of thing to build the foundation of a practice and/or to fulfill your community-service goals. However, what you need to do to build your ideal practice is to make some hard decisions.

It is important to recognize that the difficult aspect of this process is not the one where you choose which clients to target. The difficult part is choosing clients to exclude. Most of us are inclined to think, "I wouldn't want to rule out the possibility of serving that industry or that group of clients or this group of clients." However, by thinking this way, we make a fundamental mistake.

Let me relate to you the experience of a financial-services firm that does top-end work, such as issuing bonds to municipalities. This company started out by attempting to gather work of a very general nature. They began by letting it be known that they were highly specialized in any kind of financial instrument anyone could dream of, and they would be just delighted to do anything from soup to nuts in the financial world. They got exactly no response.

Then they decided to take a risk. They decided to describe their special expertise in the area of municipal bonds, and to broadcast that message instead. Within just a short period of time they had several inquiries and a few of those turned into actual mandates of considerable value.

How might their experience apply to you? Well, you can take the financial-services firm's original (rather paranoid) approach that if you exclude anyone at all from your prospect list, you might miss a client of value. Or you can take the far more effective approach of narrowing your target base to those clients you would really like to have.

Using your journal, write down the industry you would most prefer to serve and then be even more specific by listing the kinds of businesses within that industry with which you would like to work. If your situation makes it essential to target more than one industry, short-list two or three and then list a few businesses under each of them. Dare to be specific.

Learning the Tactics That Work

In order to draw up your target list of prospective clients, you may decide to employ the services of someone who can help you do the research, or you may prefer to do this on your own. Your process here is quite simple—to use the Yellow Pages or the Internet or some other system to create a list of firms or companies or families or individuals or whatever category is appropriate, people who have or may have needs of a nature that you would like to serve and may therefore fit within your business-development plan. Now let us imagine that, given your criteria, this process provides you with a list of fifty possible clients who would be attractive to you.

The next step is to prioritize these candidates. Decide who is going to be number one on that list. Who will be number fifty? Where will all the rest fit in? Put numbers beside every one of them.

Now direct your first marketing efforts *not to number one, but to number fifty*. Why? So you have the liberty of failing at the outset. You want to fail with the fiftieth candidate on your list, rather than with number one.

The best and most successful practitioners alive today learned what they know by failing, not by succeeding. Nobody learns anything by taking the easy route. People learn by the mistakes they make. "Why the heck didn't I get the work from [so-and-so]? It seemed that what we had to offer was better than what anybody else had to offer. Why didn't they choose us?"

Well, maybe they failed to choose us because they did not trust us. Maybe they failed to choose us because they did not like us. Maybe they failed to choose us because we neglected to take the time to get to know them well enough that they would be comfortable learning what we could do professionally for them. Maybe they failed to choose us because we simply did not persuade them that we were a better alternative to the provider they have now. Indeed, maybe we are *not* a better choice after all, even if we thought we were.

In Chapters 6 and 7 of this book, which dealt with very specific client-relations skills, you had an opportunity to look at the interpersonal tactics involved in courting a prospective client and meeting a prospective client. Refer back to these chapters should you feel the need, because at this point you need to examine those tactics at a strategic level.

Think of your approach in terms of army maneuvers. The strategic issues are these: With whom are we at war, and when will we engage in battle? We also need to examine the skills we bring to bear. How well will we fight when the time comes? Can we take a gun apart, clean it, put it back together again, and shoot it very straight? This all translates into deciding precisely the kind of practice you want and how you are going to get it. It further suggests that you can use trial and error to revise approaches that are not working for you.

Seeking Feedback

Turning back to the target client list, you have now numbered the individuals on the list. You know who number one is, you know who number fifty is, and you know the order of those in between. Now you need a strategic plan for approaching those prospective clients.

Your strategy at this point consists of developing a plan to go out and make actual contact with those potential clients—at a reasonable, workable pace. Again, remember that the most important part of the process is what you learn from each engagement.

It is instructive to consider those times in the past when you have not been chosen by a prospective client to whom you may have suggested some services. Have you ever considering going back to that prospective client to ask, "Why didn't you choose us?" or perhaps, "Why did you select the firm you did? What appealed to you about that firm? What was special about what you thought they could do for you?"

This is a delicate subject. You may be thinking, "How would one do that without offending that individual, or without seeming inappropriate or self-serving?" Well, many good professionals can do that with some diplomacy. They are able to say something like, "I very much respect the decision you've made to retain another firm, and I want to make it absolutely clear that I'm not here to debate that or to ask you to reconsider that. I fully accept your decision. I would simply like to learn from it, and I am wondering if you would take a couple of moments with me just to help me see what I can glean from the way you made your decision and what appealed to you about the offer you did accept."

It is true that the individual may say, "No, I don't have two minutes for you." In that case, you can retreat. However, the chances of that happening are about one in four thousand. Most of those prospective clients will be delighted to talk to you.

The Strategic Approach

Your approach is to establish and follow a plan of action that allows you, at a reasonable pace for you, to make contact with prospective clients—securing those you can as clients and then taking a moment to ask them why they decided to choose you, and being rejected by others and finding out from them why they took the path they did.

Through this process, you will begin to build two things: one, your confidence that you are developing the skill of dealing with prospective clients; and two, your knowledge base as to how prospective clients make decisions, and which of their selection methods are relevant to you.

If you start at prospect number fifty and work up the list on a consistent basis, by the time you get very far up the list you will discover that your success rate—i.e., the likelihood of a prospective client's saying "yes" instead of "no"—will consistently increase.

Chapter 36

Dealing with Rejection

Elsewhere in this book we talked about how we might say "no." At this point, let us take a look at how we feel when someone says "no" to us. Dealing with a "no" is perhaps the most fundamentally important part of the business-development process.

As lawyers we are trained to be right. When we draft a document, we expect it to be upheld if it is tested in a court (granted, not all of our documents are upheld all the time, but they should have a darned good possibility of being upheld if tested). When we draft a pleading, we expect it to be worthy of the kind of remedy that might be available to us if the facts support our argument. So we are used to doing things to perfection. We are not used to failing. In fact, if I said to you, "I know a lawyer you could hire who could work with you," and then I assured you that five or six out of ten of the documents that this lawyer drafted would be upheld if tested, you would laugh. You would have no interest in even making the acquaintance of such an individual, let alone hiring him or her.

And yet now, in the business-development area, you are about to go out and be rejected. You are about to go out and be wrong. You are about to go out and make mistake after mistake. Unless you see unhappy moments of rejection as opportunities to learn, and to improve in such a way that you achieve a level of skill that will allow you to be effective and get fewer and fewer rejections, you will not be successful at business development.

"No" Versus "No"

Obviously there are times when "no" really does mean "no," and must be accepted as such. This is the point at which you might employ the line of questioning suggested in the previous chapter, in order to find out why the client or prospective client decided to go a different route.

There are other times, however, when "no" does not mean "no." In the course of discussions with prospective clients, in the course of your efforts to be selected to do specific work, in the course of trying to persuade, where appropriate, someone to try your services where they may benefit from your assistance, you may get an interim "no" or some other response that you might easily perceive to be a "no."

You may hear, for example, "Well, I don't really think we're in a position to retain someone to do that kind of work for us at the present time."

Most people will interpret that kind of statement to be a "no." They will say to themselves, "I think at this stage I should politely leave the room without offending anybody, and try to preserve what dignity I have left."

When highly successful practitioners encounter situations on that level of difficulty—or even far more difficult situations—they respond with such questions as, "All right. Just so I understand your thinking on this, are you saying that you don't think that this is a time-sensitive concern, or are you saying that you don't think you would ever want to invest in avoiding a concern of this nature? I just want to understand your thinking."

More often than not, at the point where you assume that you have received a rejection, if you question a client or prospective client you will receive additional information which can be used very effectively to develop the relationship. For example, if the individual says, "To be candid, we're in a very tight budgetary process and we've allocated all the budget we can for legal services this year. Even though I think the risk you've warned me about is a significant one, and even though I think in a perfect world we should invest in avoiding it, I'm really hamstrung. I don't have the scope within my existing budget to move right now. That's why I don't think we can proceed."

You might respond to that kind of a statement with the following: "Tell me a little bit about your budgetary process. When is the end of your fiscal period? When might you have funds available again to invest in legal services? Is this something that may be important enough to invest in from next year's budget? If we were able as a firm to defer our billing for the two and a quarter months it will take until you're into your next fiscal period, would that make this potentially possible?"

This illustration may sound somewhat optimistic, but the important point to keep in mind is that those professionals who are unceasingly curious and who ask questions and continually learn what is going on in the minds of their clients or prospective clients are able to develop options. You may decide that in your situation it is in your best interests to leave well enough alone, and not to pursue an alternative like the one proposed above. However, if you want to win in the business-development game—if you want to win when it comes to managing opportunities and dealing with prospective clients—then you may find that, rather than taking the first "no" or "near no" as a negative response, you can discover benefits in the tactic of using that response as a springboard from which to ask questions, get further information, and develop an opportunity to offer different or more relevant alternatives. You may even find that using strategies of this nature will catapult you forward in your aspiration to achieve a better practice.

Chapter 37

Your Personal Business Advisors

In your business-development efforts, you may find it very helpful to learn from people you respect in a variety of fields. You may decide to consult with these individuals in groups or, in the case of particularly valued individuals, one-on-one in a mentoring relationship.

Advisory Boards

Some professionals put together what they call advisory boards. These are not formal boards in any sense, but rather are groups of people who are assembled by a professional because of the high respect or regard that professional has for them. An advisory board might be comprised of a few clients who are well respected, and might include some people from other professions—individuals who are highly regarded for their business and/or professional competencies.

These advisory boards may be called together for a dinner, and perhaps given a small gift to take home afterwards. The purpose of the meeting is to ask the advisory board to listen for a little while to the professional. The professional takes the opportunity to talk about the kinds of things he or she would like to achieve in the business-development area, the kinds of efforts that he or she has expended to date, and the kinds of results that have been experienced.

The professional then asks the advisory board, "Any thoughts? Ideas? Suggestions? Criticisms? Encouragements?"

After this, the advisors are given a freewheeling opportunity to offer some advice.

Most such advisory boards turn out to be highly constructive. As Robert Cialdini suggests in *Influence* regarding the power of asking others for help and/or advice, as a result of such meetings the board members tend to become very much interested and focused in your success. You will find them following up with you and asking, "Well, how is it going? Have you achieved what you hoped to achieve?" In fact, you may find that if you fail to get together with them often enough, they will be asking, "When are we getting together again? I'd be interested to find out how you're doing."

Assembling this kind of personal advisory board is one tactic that many professionals find extremely helpful. Make a quick list in your journal of a few candidates for your advisory board. Having specific individuals in mind may help you decide if this idea is right for you.

Mentors

Another tactic that you may find very helpful, not only for business development but for your practice management as well, is to choose a mentor.

A mentor is someone you believe has knowledge or experience that may be useful to you, that may save you some trial and error, and save you some failures. For the relationship to work effectively, the mentor should be someone in whom you have confidence—and it should also be someone for whom you have some affection, because dealing with that individual should be enjoyable as well as productive. The mentor also by definition needs to be someone who has some interest in your career, your achievement, and your success.

The best mentoring relationships are highly customized. The effective use of a mentor involves communicating candidly at the outset about what you hope to achieve. By telling an individual that you have a lot of regard for their experience, their success, and their knowledge, and that you think you would greatly benefit from some opportunity to interact with them, you will set the stage. The initial feedback will tell you whether that person is interested in fulfilling the role.

If the individual is interested in working with you, you should establish a pattern or frequency of getting together that seems right for the two of you. Like everything else, a productive relationship of this nature requires some discipline: it may evaporate if you do not find some way to ensure that it continues. You might, for example, decide on a number of meetings over the course of the next year, simultaneously recording them in your respective diaries, and then adhering to that meeting schedule.

This scheduling strategy seems like a very simple tactic, too simple to mention perhaps, but it is important. Even well-wishing mentors and protégés often find that after a highly productive get-together, nothing happens for several months. They realize, "Gee, as I think about it, neither of us really took the time to decide when we're going to get together next." That approach—or lack of it, to be more precise—is simply not going to help you accomplish what you need and want to accomplish.

Chapter 38

The Power of Appreciation

I am constantly amazed at the number of lawyers who get referrals from existing clients or bankers or other people, and do not say "Thank you." When I ask those lawyers, "How did you express your appreciation for that referral?" they will look at me quizzically and say something in a defensive tone, like, "Well, we go to dinner occasionally," or "I'm fairly sure I referred something to *them* one time last year."

Behavioral-conditioning experiments have shown us that if we want the puppy to come to us when we ring the bell the next time, we have to provide a reward when the puppy responds to the bell this time. It is pretty straightforward: If you want more of the same behavior, reinforce it. If you want less, fail to reinforce it. In the client context, showing appreciation with a thank-you card or even just a phone call can be extremely powerful in reinforcing and making more consistent the behavior you want. It also helps you to avoid the tremendous potential fallout from failing to do anything.

How many times have you done a favor for someone and later realized that they never thanked you? How many times have you said to yourself, "That's the last time I stick my neck out for that person"?

Well, your client may feel exactly the same way about you. They stuck their neck out. They made a referral to you. They took a chance. If the person they referred is unhappy with you, they could find themselves in trouble with a relationship that is important to them. The least we can do for that kind of investment on their part is to express appreciation.

In regard to the method of saying "thank you," one tactic is becoming increasingly powerful in this day and age—and that is the handwritten note. People used to write letters all the time, but in today's highly electronic age where voices and electronic impulses and words flash across screens, the intimacy of a handwritten note has become even more eloquent than it used to be because of its increasing rarity. In fact, if you melt a little wax on the back and do an imprint of your insignia, you may really astound the recipient. Wax or no wax, however, if this personal communication strategy appeals to you, you can easily obtain some stationery that already says "Thank You" on it, whether it is generic stock or a card that is embossed with the name of your firm. You should do this soon. Having a supply within reach is important, because only if it is very, very easy are you likely to do it. We all know that if writing a note requires a special effort, the next client file will probably get in the way.

Appreciation Within the Office

I have mentioned elsewhere that as lawyers we usually do not feel overly appreciated at work. As we all know, under-appreciated lawyers, or those who feel under-appreciated, are susceptible to being headhunted away. Many good lawyers who change firms do not do so simply for the money.

Members of support staffs, like lawyers, tend to be quite hungry for appreciation. When I have had the opportunity to talk to members of support staffs of some very good firms, they are usually very loyal to the firm and very positive, but in a moment of confidence and trust they may explain that there are times when they are a little disheartened. The firm might have some very tight policies or rules, for example, or simply have senior people who tend to offer negative feedback about incidents such as leaving early on occasion, or taking a personal phone call. The support staff member says, "Nobody remembers that I stayed three hours late three nights in a row last week to get the share issue done for the securities department."

If we allow the members of our support staffs to think that we are police officers who look for any variance from policy so that we can dish out—politely or not so politely—a little bit of negative reinforcement, we will certainly not get peak performances from them. People do expect to be noticed—and want to be noticed—when they go beyond the scope of their duty. You may want to consider making it a habit that when you observe a member of the support staff doing something extraordinary—staying late, working very hard, getting something done extremely well—you take a moment to convey some appreciation.

Sometimes we fail to show appreciation or give positive feedback because—yet again—we are too caught up in the analytical and critical approach to our work product. Again this may be understandable, but it is not likely the best strategy.

Let me give you an illustration. A junior person or a member of the support staff drafts a letter for me and brings it into my office. I look the letter over and find it is not too bad at all—except that in the third paragraph on the second page a reference to a legal issue appears that makes me uncomfortable. I feel this reference does not properly reflect the issue. I think the paragraph needs to be fine-tuned. So I provide a little feedback to the person who drafted the letter, saying, "This paragraph suffers from being a little vague and I really need to tighten that up to properly explain . . . [whatever]."

Let us look at the way I have responded in the context of the whole letter. How was the paragraph that opened the correspondence? It was quite good—it was cordial, it was friendly, and it was pretty effective. What about the second paragraph, which summarized the events over the past month? That was quite good, too. That was accurate. But did I say so? No. I focused immediately on what needed to be fixed—on what could be better.

As you get work from those who produce it for you, remind yourself to first look for what was done well—even if it was only a small part. Your feedback will then sound something like this: "Thank you for doing this work. I like the opening very much. I think the review of what we've done previously was very strong, very well communicated. I have a small concern about the way the legal issue is expressed on the second page, and this is what I intend to do about it. Thank you for the letter."

That is how you convey appreciation to people. That is how you avoid circumstances where people say, "The only thing anyone ever notices around here is when I make a mistake, and then they're ready to jump on it. When I do something right, I never hear about it."

Appreciation is probably the most powerful human communications tool. Used effectively, not only with clients but with those lawyers and support staff with whom you work, and who work so hard for you, even small investments of appreciation are likely to provide you with enormous returns. Consider a daily addition to your to-do list—add the name of one person to whom you will communicate appreciation.

Chapter 39

Multidiscipline Groups

A tactic that many professionals have used to their advantage in their business-development initiatives is to assemble a group of individuals from a diverse set of professions or industries who get together from time to time—maybe once a month for breakfast—to share information and to teach each other about their respective worlds.

The idea here is to find people you respect from various disciplines, and to get them together to create a resource group of mutual benefit. You can ask, "Would it make sense for us to get together once a month or so? We could take turns leading the meeting, and the person whose responsibility it is to lead each time would provide some useful information about their profession or industry that may be of interest to others. We could get to know each other a little better, and we might even occasionally make referrals to each other that could be helpful." (Most groups find such referrals happen informally, by the way, and that it is not necessary to make them a requirement of participation.)

You will not need to build the whole group yourself; those you invite will have friends, associates, and acquaintances they will want to include as well. You can begin with a core group and expand, as people within the group suggest other people from other professions. One pretty decent rule for such groups is that they include only one person from each industry or profession.

Benefits of participating in such groups include the perspectives with which the other members of the group provide you, which may be helpful to your clients as well as to yourself. Clients tend to see lawyers as fairly linear, as contained within certain technical areas of expertise.

The suggestions you can give your clients by virtue of your awareness of a number of different industries and professions can give those clients a very positive impression regarding your approach. You will find it serves you very well for clients to perceive you as refreshingly diverse, well rounded, and balanced.

In addition, there is often much going on in other organizations that is foreign to your operations, but which can be very helpful. For example, imagine for a moment the value to a law firm in learning how to deal with potential public relations crises from risk management experts. Even some of the best law firms in the world may suddenly encounter some great difficulty—perhaps an embarrassing lawsuit against a partner for harassment or theft or some other scandal. As lawyers, we are normally ill-prepared to deal with such crises. Exchanging ideas on a consistent basis with other professionals from other walks of life can give us an ongoing source of insight into how other people deal with situations we may suddenly need to face—not to mention providing us with a place to go to seek advice if we need it in a hurry. These are some of the by-product benefits of being a member of a multidisciplinary group.

Whether for the immediate benefit of referrals from people in other professions and disciplines, or in order to learn new things for your own personal satisfaction or for your firm's advancement or protection, or to develop an image that is more appealing to your clients, you will find it beneficial to invest some of your time getting together with people from other professions and other industries to exchange knowledge and ideas.

Chapter 40

Becoming More Profitable

You owe it to yourself to read David Maister's book *Managing the Professional Service Firm.* In the portions of it that deal with profitability, Maister covers a number of issues that can serve you well in terms of enhancing your bottom line.

Among other initiatives, Maister includes quite a sophisticated analysis of a formula that derives profits per partner. In essence, he uses equations that deal with the following four elements:

- Leverage—meaning, in this context, the work we do through others (note that "others" might include technology);
- Rates—our traditional hourly rates;
- Utilization—how many hours we work, or rather those work hours for which we get paid; and
- Margins—the ratio of our revenue against our costs.

New practitioners who are building practices may find that their challenge is simply to get some billable hours in the door. They are less worried about the sophistication of the work at that stage, or its conformance to their career goals—they simply want to attract some work. In some practices, too, the issue of margin is fundamental to the direction taken by the lawyers in the firm. If costs are absolutely astronomical—if every lawyer has 10,000 square feet, for example—then that problem has to be addressed through billings. However, if a reasonable amount of work is coming through the door and costs are fairly well contained, some real magic can occur in the areas of leverage and rates.

Rates

Later in this book I am going to deal with billing and finances, and as part of that discussion I will discuss "hourly rates" versus "value billing." For now, let us look at rates in their own right, and think about how they affect profitability.

The first question we must ask ourselves is this: Why would intelligent people who have a range of choices decide to pay us more per hour next year than they are paying us this year? The answer to that question is that they will do this because they recognize our value to them. One of the reasons we consistently want to increase our value to our clients is to be allowed to charge higher rates.

In an early chapter, I made reference to an individual who is so specialized as a chemist and a lawyer that the large petroleum companies hire him when they have laboratory accidents or risky situations. You need to identify what it is about *you* that makes you special enough that you are able to command higher rates.

Many lawyers tend to dissociate themselves from this discussion. They will say something like, "I do mainly real-estate work and there's no room for achieving higher rates in that area. That work is essentially perceived as a commodity—in fact, I am constantly under pressure from my clients to lower and lower my fees."

Someone in this situation might consider such questions as these:

1. Which aspects of the real-estate work I am doing are routine, and which aspects are not routine? Have I had some unusual success in dealing with easement issues, for example, or taxation issues relating to property?
2. Can I segregate the "unusual" portion of my practice from the more routine work—work relating to title acquisition, for example?

If the answer to such questions is "yes," this person may be able to carve out for themselves an area of specialty that is compatible with, or can co-exist with, the routine or commodity work they are doing, in such a way that they can offer "blended" or "multiple" rates. Some lawyers are able to command enormous rates for highly specialized situations that arise from routine areas of practice.

It would be very difficult within the scope of this book to set out all of the specific applications of this principle; there are endless combinations and permutations of practice areas and opportunities. In order to determine how the principle applies to your practice, ask your-self such questions as the following:

- Are there areas where I can be of greater value—at least to some clients?
- If so, how can I get to those areas?
- How can I communicate to potential clients the kind of work I do?

Then think about carving out special rates for those special tasks.

Leverage

Leverage traditionally has been the ratio of partners to nonpartners in a firm. At this point, I invite you to consider leverage in a slightly dif-ferent way—a nontraditional way that you will find applicable whether you are a sole practitioner, partner, or non-partner. Leverage for you should be *the manner in which you get work done without imposing your personal time.*

For many individuals this definition of leverage involves the use of technology. The subject of technology vis à vis the practice of law will be dealt with more extensively in the following chapter, but in terms of its relationship to profitability, technology can be seen as a way of cre-ating work product more effectively and more efficiently with an in-vestment of less effort and less time.

Going a step or two beyond that, some lawyers have learned how to use technology to create packaged product.

What is "packaged product" for a lawyer? Here is one example: A law firm that deals in the area of employment law or industrial rela-tions has created for its clients and prospective clients a package of tools that clients can use internally for both training and for auditing risk. The magic of that course of action is that the package can be sold for a fixed price—and it does not have to be reproduced every single time.

If your area of practice is fraught with processes or procedures that are repeatable, then you may be able to create a similar package.

Again, some of you may say, "You just don't understand how idio-syncratic my practice is, and how unique each situation is. I couldn't possibly create anything that would be repeatable. I don't think this ap-plies to me."

Consider this—when you are advising clients, or writing your opinions, or presenting to groups of clients or prospective clients in your area of expertise, or when you are creating checklists that you may use internally on cases, or even checklists that you give to clients in order for them to give you appropriate instructions, are there not pieces or parts that are repeatable?

One physician I know of has made a videotape explaining the procedures and risks involved in certain medical situations. Obviously, this goes to the issue of consent for medical procedures, and he has done this partly to reduce risk from an insurance point of view. But beyond that, is there an analogy for your practice? Is there some part of the advice or the recommendations you give in conducting processes related to your legal matters that is repeatable? Is there some part that a client could actually observe using some media—rather than needing to be one-on-one, personally present, face-to-face with you?

Imagine for a moment saying to the client, "Take this CD-ROM with you and have a look at some of the issues presented on it, and let me know if anything arises from it that is of concern to you." Imagine the saving of time and the enhancement of quality. Imagine the competitive advantage.

Think of one area in which you could employ this tactic and make a note of it in your journal.

Working Smart

Before leaving the area of leverage, let us consider the opportunity to get intelligent people among our support staffs to carry out more functions—thereby freeing the lawyers in the firm to get more done per hour.

One firm has taken a step in this regard which I find quite remarkable. This firm went out and hired college graduates who had absolutely no legal training—no law school, no legal experience whatsoever. These people were hired because they were smart. They could identify issues and they could assimilate information very quickly.

Next, the firm built some systems for getting certain kinds of work done in such areas, for example, as corporations and probate work. With respect to each one of those systems, they plugged in the component tasks and said, "Does it take a law degree to do that task? When we do corporate work, for example, we do not require a lawyer to look through the minute book to see if the directors have changed. Anybody who is smart and can assimilate information can do that." They handed that kind of work over to their new employees.

As your practice becomes more technologically proficient, as you acquire better document-generating tools, as you develop better systems and processes, ask yourself consistently whether there are pieces or parts of that work where your specialized training as a lawyer is not required. Are there aspects of your routine work that some smart person with appropriate education and experience could learn to do, and do with quality?

Real Support, Virtual Relationships

In the past we have thought of support personnel as people that we put behind a desk or behind a computer terminal somewhere in our organization—which involves another so many square feet, another benefits package, and so on. Today many firms are realizing the advantages of having "virtual" relationships with support workers. Today many people may be available who are smart and capable of assisting you in your cause who may not need to occupy space in your physical premises. They may not need to have a lot of face-to-face interaction with you. They may do quite well using their skills, their knowledge, and their technology in some other place.

You are probably aware of some of the experiments where work has been done in one country rather than another because of the costs involved. I am not referring here to the production of tangible goods, I am referring to the processing of data. Some significant experiments are underway where data is being processed in India for American corporations, for example, and is being transmitted back and forth on the Internet. As this book is being written an Internet site has appeared that offers voice-to-text services especially for lawyers and doctors: A lawyer or doctor can simply use the telephone or voice-to-text equipment, send it along as a file on the Internet, and within three hours the voice is converted to text—without that lawyer or doctor having to train the equipment at all.

These kinds of services and opportunities are going to mushroom very quickly over the next few years. The challenge for you is to determine how you can utilize smart people who have appropriate skills and experience in a way that allows you to get more work done, using less of your time.

More Balance, Better Work

Recently, at a large firm gathering, a managing partner shared a revelation he had had. He said, "It occurs to me that it isn't simply working more hours or working harder that is going to get us more profitability. In and of themselves, working more hours and working harder simply give us more stress, more anxiety, and add more burdens to our shoulders. The key is to find ways of *doing work we love, for people we enjoy serving, for which we can command significant rates*. Then we can make the same living or even improve our standards of living without working harder."

I encourage you to reflect on that partner's revelation. How can you work smarter and not harder? How can you find ways to be more valuable, command better rates or, through leverage, create packaged products or other processes that save you time? By doing so, you will command more income while at the same time carving off more of your life for your family and other things you want to do. You will allow yourself to achieve some balance.

People who achieve a balance in their lives come to work with greater enthusiasm, and can give much more per hour than others—and by doing so, they increase their value even further.

Chapter 41

Harnessing Technology

Recently I had the opportunity to talk to a litigator who is quite famous—you would recognize his name if I told it to you—and he said with some pride that he does not use any technology to assist him in retrieving information from transcripts during the discovery process.

Now, as all readers of this book will know, in the course of a long discovery thousands of pages of transcripts are produced. And if technology can allow us to find every reference to a particular issue at the stroke of a finger—at the speed of light—then let me ask you this question: Would you want to retain a lawyer to represent you who did not make use of that technology?

Why is it that so many senior, powerful law practitioners are so proud to announce that they do not know how to make a copy of a document? Why do others mention so complacently that they really do not understand technology, or know how to use it—although they certainly admire those who do? This situation is not unique to the profession of law. In a recent article describing CEOs of top companies, it was revealed that the extent of the lack of knowledge regarding technology among executives was amazing.

Some of you have already embraced technology. Some of you love it. Some of you cannot wait to get your hands on—and your minds around—the next new technological tool, device, or methodology. However, others have an aversion to the whole area, and I believe that their reluctance to become involved is going to cost them dearly in the years ahead. For them, I would like to offer some practical guidelines that will allow them to appreciate the most basic, reasonable access to technology and implementation of technology that should be applied to the practice of law today.

If there is one piece of advice I would give to brand new lawyers that would be far more important than anything else I might offer, it would be that they should begin tracking information from day one—and never stop. Whether you are using a handheld device or something far more sophisticated in a supercomputer does not really matter; the point is that with a computer, you can track and retain all kinds of valuable information.

People and Documents

Database technology allows us to keep track of every contact and every person we meet, and to retain notes on every attribute of those people that is significant to us at the time. Our databases should include information relating to such people as our clients, individuals who refer other individuals to us, people in related professions and industries, other lawyers who may have expertise or experience that is relevant to us, and so on. When we capture this data technologically, we can retrieve it when we need it.

Similarly, we should store in a computerized format all the work that we produce. It takes very little technology to capture every document, every letter, every checklist, and so on. In our own organization recently, one of us asked another whether he happened to have a document that we had created five years ago. It is no exaggeration to say that it took about 35 seconds to find that document among 36,000 files, and to produce a replica of it. Five or ten years ago, that would have been impossible. In the near future, it will be a minimum requirement.

In addition to our individual databases, we need to be able to capture the precedents that are being created within the firm so that they are accessible instantly by those who would benefit from having access to them. Today, increasingly sophisticated document-generation systems are allowing the authors of documents in precedent databases to make them even more useful by adding "Help" boxes, so that those who are less sophisticated or less experienced can obtain information from experts within their own firm when they come to a decision point that is challenging for them—and to do this electronically, without talking to them directly.

There is one problem with this type of firmwide data collection. In many cases, when you try to obtain the precedents that should go into such a system from the professionals in the firm, they will tell you that they really do not have anything good enough to go into it at the moment. They will tell you that they need to review a few things, take another look. They will promise to do that and get back to you. (I have always found such statements ironic. I mean, what did they sell to their clients yesterday that is not good enough to go into the firm's precedent bank today?) As a result, the only way to get good precedents into a system is to have a means or a process whereby the support staff can "steal" them as they are produced and put them into the system.

Having said that, however, we must also address the issue of quality control, especially over important documentation. Today many firms are adopting the concept of a "gatekeeper" for that purpose. The gatekeeper is an individual who alone can decide whether a document can be modified within the knowledge bank of the firm.

Keeping Up with the Clients

I began this chapter by talking about our attitudes as lawyers toward technology, attitudes that no doubt are based on our individual experiences. However, the way we feel about technology is becoming less and less relevant. Today, technology is being driven by the clients, not the lawyers.

Most sophisticated clients today demand of their law firms that they have highly advanced systems in place that will allow text, audio, and visual information to pass back and forth easily. Large corporate clients may also demand advanced networking systems that allow the sharing of information with other firms that are serving those clients at the same time. Legal work in this day and age also demands that we have secure and highly refined knowledge-management systems. (This sounds like jargon to the uninitiated, but it is really very basic. "Knowledge management" simply means capturing our work so that we can retrieve it at will, in an organized manner.)

If concepts and systems like the ones I have been discussing here sound like they belong on *Star Trek*, it is time to make use of the technological expertise available to you, and to learn from it. The successful lawyer of the future will embrace technology, will understand it, and will know how to exploit it.

Part VI

Fundamentals and Finance

Chapter 42

Billing and Finance

One of the dumbest things that the legal profession ever did was to decide to bill on an hourly basis. This notion was totally misconceived.

You might well ask, "If the notion was so misconceived, why did lawyers do it?" The reasons are worth explaining.

Many years ago, lawyers used to bill their files by picking them up and feeling them and sensing how heavy they were, and wondering what the client could afford, and wondering how good the advice was that was offered—ultimately coming up with an amount based largely on intuition, and then billing that amount to the client.

Then someone came along who decided it might be worthwhile to explore whether junior lawyers were adding profit to the partners of the firm. They came up with a method of analysis which went something like this: "Suppose that our junior lawyer works 1,200 hours a year, and suppose that the cost rate or margin rate in our firm is 50 percent—in other words, suppose that costs equal 50 percent of revenues received by the firm. Further, suppose that we pay the junior lawyer $60,000 per year. How much will the junior lawyer need to bill in order to cost us nothing and make us nothing—to be cost-neutral?"

A simple calculation revealed that the junior lawyer would need to bill $100 per hour. So the members of this firm decided that they would begin to measure and track how many hours the junior worked on each file, so that when they billed the file they could figure out whether or not they had retrieved the cost of the junior lawyer. This practice spread, and after a while it became part of the billing practice of the firm. And when that happened, they discovered that the income of those lawyers who recorded their time and billed on a time basis increased by 40 percent.

Well, as you can imagine, the impact of this finding was rather powerful. A 40 percent boost in income, simply for recording time? The practice spread like wildfire.

Only one small problem existed, and that was that this ingenious way of tracking costs soon became established as the exclusive means of setting price. Can you think of another industry or profession besides ours that has demonstrated to the client all of the internal calculations and made them available and made them visible, thereby allowing them to be managed from the outside? Those who practice in the insurance area and some other areas know just how sophisticated outside management of lawyers has become. The in-house counsel of some corporations go to school to learn how to better manage their outside lawyers, and they set stringent guidelines that range from allowable disbursements to the hourly rates that are acceptable, depending on years of call.

Time Versus Value

I will explain why an hourly billing methodology is misconceived.

Let us imagine that a lawyer needs to produce a sophisticated document for a sophisticated situation, and it takes that lawyer twenty-five hours to do the work at—let us choose a random billing rate of $300 an hour—a cost of $7,500. What does the lawyer charge for that document? Well, if the traffic will bear it, if the client is wealthy enough and careless enough to pay anything it needs to pay, the lawyer may be successful in retrieving the $7,500.

Now the next client comes along and needs a similar document. This time it takes the lawyer two hours to produce the document, because only a few modifications to the previous document are required. How much does the lawyer bill? Six hundred dollars—for a similar situation to the one for which the lawyer has just charged another client $7,500. Does that make sense? Well of course not.

In short, the rational approach to billing is not based on hours. It is based on value.

The Client's Perspective

Ironically, clients are clamoring for value-based billing. Not in so many words, perhaps; their approach is not so much that value-based is better than time-based billing. Their perspective is that they want some certainty ahead of time in terms of what the bill is going to be. Clients want to budget for their legal services. Whether they are individuals or the largest corporations in the world, they want to know, "What is it going to cost?"

The relevance of this to your practice is as follows: Unless you are in one of those practice areas like basic insurance defense law where your client has become extremely sophisticated at managing you from the outside, based on your hourly rate and other factors—and the hourly rates of others with whom you provide the work—I suggest that you consider never again mentioning your hourly rate—or any hourly rate—to clients.

Now you may well ask, "If I never mention an hourly rate, then how in the world would I ever answer a question about what a matter might cost?" Let us look at this question from a different perspective.

Imagine that you take your automobile back to the Mercedes dealership where you acquired it because you hear a funny noise in the engine. You ask the service manager, "What do you think that noise is?"

The service manager says, "Doesn't sound good, but I think I'll need to open her up before I can really tell you what the problem is."

"Gee!" you say. "Well, what do you think this might cost me?"

"Oh, I can't say," the service manager replies. "You see, these are far too complicated situations. The years and years of experience that I've acquired as a service manager allow me to make these decisions as I go. I couldn't possibly predict a cost for you. We charge our mechanics out at $125 an hour, and so what we'll do is multiply that number by the number of hours it takes to solve the problem, and that will be what you will pay."

How comfortable would you be with an estimate of that nature? Surely, you would want to say to that service manager, "You have been repairing Mercedes-Benz vehicles for the last umpteen years . . . you've seen thousands of cars come in, you've seen thousands of cars go out. You must have *some* notion, based on your experience and skill, as to roughly what is wrong with this engine, or the range of things that might be wrong with this engine, and what it might take to resolve those problems—and by doing that, you should be able to give me a range."

This is exactly the position of our clients when they ask us what a particular matter is going to cost. It does not satisfy the client for us to say, "We change X hundreds of dollars per hour, and it just depends on how many hours it takes us geniuses to solve this problem in our own idiosyncratic way. We'll multiply the two numbers, and that's what you will pay."

When we give such a response, what does the client do? The client looks for tactics to reduce our costs. One tactic is to object to our hourly rate and to suggest it should be lower, or to suggest that some other firm might provide a lower rate, or in some other way to intimidate us into lowering that rate. A second tactic, even more insidious, is to wait until the job is done, wait until we bill, and then find something to object about in relation to the product or work we have provided. Either way, this puts us in a vulnerable situation.

Step by Step

The best practice for billing is to estimate fees based on value, on a phase-by-phase basis, as you go through the work you need to do for your client. Every matter, regardless how sophisticated, regardless how complicated, will allow you to value bill if you break it into small phases. You will find that your clients are typically much more comfortable knowing with some certainty ahead of time how much things will cost, and will be able to relate value to the service provided much more easily.

Here is a specific example: A matter comes before you that requires that you review a lot of documentation and perhaps research the law and provide a preliminary recommendation as to a course of action. You can probably predict with a great deal of accuracy how much time and effort you will expend on this. In your own calculations you can use internal hourly rates to determine what you think this phase of the work will cost you, given the way you price your services. You will then be able to assess such related issues as whether the value of the work to the client is going to exceed the hourly-based cost in such a way that you can offer that work for a premium. Conversely, you may decide that you are prepared to offer services for less than the normally billed amount where circumstances warrant it. Based on your good judgment, you can then propose to the client that you do that first phase for amount X. If the client agrees, then you may want to get a retainer.

In order to have a highly successful practice, you need to embrace billing and financial controls that will work effectively for you. By following the practices for value billing set out here, you will achieve a great deal of success both in the return on your time investments—including premiums, where appropriate—but also in terms of your clients' satisfaction levels, and their willingness to pay your fees.

Asking For Retainers

While there may be circumstances where long-standing clients have proven to be good payers of your fees and it is truly unnecessary to explore obtaining retainers from them, in many cases lawyers fail to get retainers in circumstances where they should. Retainers benefit clients as well as you and your firm. Clients like predictable cash flow, certainty, avoiding large unexpected expenses—to be candid, $5,000 per month just seems like less than $60,000 in one annual lump.

Asking for retainers is daunting to many. Perhaps glancing at a list of receivables you have written off will give you courage. The good news is that if you look a client straight in the eye and ask for a retainer, and where appropriate give payment options, you will be surprised at how receptive most clients are. Some are actually relieved.

Chapter 43

Preparing Better Accounts

The manner in which we as lawyers have traditionally billed clients, describing our services and our work in a very clinical, unexciting, unimaginative way, has been one of our Achilles' heels.

As we have been doing the work, we have been recording our time, and we have been describing how the time was spent in a fairly mundane fashion. We have noted, for example, "phone call with opposing counsel," or "obtaining documentation," or "reviewing letter."

As a result, we tend to report and create a bill that tracks information in that same way. This means that the client gets a bill that says something like, "To reviewing letters . . . To receiving phone call from you . . . To phoning another lawyer . . . To receiving another phone call from you . . . To phoning other lawyer again . . ." etc., etc., etc. This is very unexciting, unimaginative stuff.

And how does the client react to this bill? The client probably looks at it and says, "Look at this! The son of a gun charged me for every single phone call. Some of those phone calls weren't even necessary! In fact, some of those phone calls were ones I made because the lawyer wasn't keeping me up-to-date on what was happening on the case—if I hadn't phoned, I wouldn't have known what was going on." So they get irritated. Very irritated. And they may get additionally irritated by the way we charge out our disbursements.

In 1969, J. Harris Morgan—one of the pioneers of law office management—created a work for the American Bar Association entitled *Romancing Fees Into the 20th Century*, in which he proposed a very basic

209

concept. He said that what we ought to consider doing as we created our accounts for clients was to "project effort."

What he meant was that rather than just saying you phoned the other lawyer, you should say why you phoned the other lawyer, or what the benefit from the phone call was to the client. For example, where the traditional account might say, "To phoning other lawyer," J. Harris Morgan would suggest, "To phoning other lawyer to begin to negotiate an amount which might be appropriate to settle the first portion of this dispute." Or "To phoning other lawyer to obtain the information necessary in order to draft the pleading that had to be filed." Or whatever. That way, he said, the client could relate to the necessity and the benefit of that act. The whole point was to continually project effort to the client in a way the client could understand.

Many lawyers reacted to this suggestion by saying, "But isn't the client more interested in the result than in the effort? Isn't the only really important thing whether we won or lost? Whether we got the title or didn't get the title?" According to a great deal of research that J. Harris Morgan told us about, the answer—even way back then—was "no." In fact, the client cares more about your effort than about the result.

These research findings are not so unreasonable when you think about other contexts. Imagine, for example, that you have a medical situation that is not very happy, that is not going to go away completely—but your doctor has been fabulous. Your doctor has kept you informed. Your doctor is well-skilled, well-educated and well-trained. Your doctor is a renowned expert in his or her field and has done his or her very best for you, and in addition has been attentive to you and is still following up with you. Are you happy with your doctor? Yes, you are. You believe you have the right doctor working on your team.

Conversely, imagine another situation in which your doctor is aloof, arrogant, and uncommunicative—but is, indeed, able to solve some medical problem for you. Do you love that doctor? Are you going to refer others to that doctor? No. You tolerate a doctor like that because you have no other choice. You are relieved with the result, but you have no affection or appreciation for that doctor at all.

Now apply these analogies to our own profession.

In the client-relations segment of this book, we discussed how we might attract more appreciation and client satisfaction from those we serve. Our billing process is an integral part of doing that. If we bill in a manner that shows that we care about our clients and that we trust them to understand and appreciate relevant information, in which we show our clients in relevant and realistic terms the effort we have expended—not with hyperbole, not with exaggeration, but in a straightforward, adult-to-adult manner—we will find that we have clients who are far more likely, and more willing, to pay our bills.

Chapter 44

Financial Discipline

Ask yourself some questions about the financial systems currently in place in your law firm.

- Do those systems alert you when your work-in-progress exceeds certain predetermined amounts?
- Do they let you know when disbursements exceed prespecified limits?
- Do they warn you when work-in-progress begins to get "old" and is still unbilled?
- Do they tell you when an account that has been rendered has not been paid within a reasonable period of time?
- Do they prevent those who work with you from reducing bills, without appropriate approvals, below what you have agreed is the cost of producing the work?

These financial protocols and systems are "best practices" of some of the most successful firms in the world. In fact, in some firms, if you have not billed on a matter where work-in-progress is aging, a bill will be rendered for you. It will not be sent directly to the client—it will come to your desk as a draft, and your options will be to fine-tune it and send it out, or to make your plea to the management or executive committee or billing committee as to why your bill should be exempted from the bills going out that month.

In many of the firms I have served, partners will say, "Oh, I believe in financial discipline. In fact, I believe you should have all of these systems in place, and I believe you should follow all of the protocols you've described. Just make sure you never do that when it relates to one of my clients. You see, my clients are different. They're special. You'd have to know a lot more about them to understand them than I can tell you right now. So, sure, put your systems in place, but don't make them apply to my clients."

Well, I think you would probably agree that this approach is not going to be successful. The only exception for going around the system that might be valid would occur if a partner promises the firm that for a specific client, bills will be rendered, work-in-progress will not be allowed to age, receivables will be monitored, and so on. As long as that financial discipline continues, then that client may be exempted from the firm-wide systems. Otherwise, for systems to work, they need to be universal.

Chapter 45

Overcoming Fee Resistance

People today are growing accustomed to getting better and better value for their money. They are increasingly comfortable with negotiating. They are used to determining whether they are getting the very best price for any given product or service.

If you are purchasing a computer in a store, the first thing you want to know is whether you are getting the best price available for that computer. You may ask questions of the salesperson about the given price such as, "Is it possible that this computer could be acquired for a little less than [X]?" or "Are there any circumstances in which that price might be reduced? Is the price flexible? Might this go on sale?" or "Might there be an opportunity to get a better rate than [X] on this one when a newer version comes along?"

Whatever your specific questions, you are basically asking, "Is this the best I can do?"

A trained salesperson will look you straight in the eye and with great confidence will say something to this effect: "Number one, let me assure you that the particular computer you are considering is the very best model available on Planet Earth. Number two, the usual price for this model is astronomical. In fact, it is normally priced at [Y]. Anywhere else you try to acquire this, you'd be looking at [Y] plus plus, or even more. Because of our tremendous ability to acquire these products in great volume [or whatever the story is], we are in a position to offer you unique value. You will never find this for less anywhere else."

There may even be a guarantee offered to the effect that if you find this same model for less within a certain period of time, the store will return double the difference to you, or something to that effect.

In short, you will get a very strong assurance from the computer salesperson. You will walk out of that situation believing that you have secured a very good deal—and often you will have.

Now let us look at the same situation in a law-firm setting. You estimate a price. Your client looks at you and says, "Gee, that's a lot of money. It's really a lot more than I had budgeted for, and I'm really concerned about that." Or perhaps he or she says, "My CEO is concerned about our expending money in this way. Is there any possibility that we could do this for a little less?" Or something of that nature.

What do we do?

Well, what we do not typically do is give that client an assurance. We do not usually look the client in the eye and assure him or her of the merits of our estimate. Instead, we tend to become frightened. What if we lose the client? What if they select someone else? With those fears in mind, we either capitulate on the spot, or we say we would like to talk to our management committee—and then we run to our partners and suggest to them that we really ought to lower our fees because otherwise we might lose the client.

I am not suggesting that this is not a highly competitive world. I know it is. There may be times when you need to exercise personal judgment and even perhaps in certain cases to lower or moderate your fees. However, rather than responding reflexively with fear, we should learn first to apply the same tactic that the computer salesperson applied—and that is to assure clients that they are getting good value. We need to assure clients that we are uniquely well equipped to deal with their challenges, their problems, and their situations, and that we are deploying the very best people available within our firm to assist them. We need to assure them, too, that the fee that is being asked is very much commensurate with the value that they will receive. We may even want to add where appropriate that, due to efficiencies and effective systems, the fee is likely lower than some other professional firms would need to charge to provide the same value.

At that point, the client may very well do what we do often in a showroom when we are buying a product, and that is to accept the explanation. If this does not happen, then we need to apply personal judgment as to how to proceed from there. Obviously, there are some times when we will need to negotiate in order to resolve fee problems with our clients in a mutually satisfactory manner.

The important point to note is that all too often, we capitulate far too early. All too often, we fail even to demonstrate that we have confidence in the fees that we are charging. All too often, by capitulating so early we probably reinforce the client behavior of questioning our fees—and make the client think, "I guess the name of the game is that whatever the law firm suggests by way of fees, you complain a little and you say it's painful and then they moderate the amount." It becomes a conditioned response.

There are two points of vulnerability in terms of billing and our financial relationship with clients. One is when we estimate our fees, and the other is when we render our bills. Successful lawyers learn how to manage the expectations of their clients, and they also show confidence when it comes to fees and value.

Chapter 46

Managing Time

Several years ago, a very distinguished presenter pointed out to an audience that the phrase "time management" is a misnomer—after all, time is not manageable at all. He reminded his listeners that the Pope, heads of state, your favorite movie star, your favorite athlete, all have exactly the same number of hours in a day as you do.

Time cannot be managed. What we *can* do is to allocate and use time effectively.

As lawyers we tend to be perfectionists. We feel we must do everything exactly right. That attitude can get us into some trouble. While it is true that we should not be providing documentation or agreements to clients that are shoddy or haphazard, there are diminishing returns—as we all know—if we spend too long considering every word. Certainly when it comes to such initiatives as our business-development activities, if we wait at each phase until we have perfected it, we will die before we get to where we want to go.

There is a creature with which I think most of us are familiar that can be referred to as the "mental-block" case. Perhaps the account on the file is going to be somewhat larger than your client was expecting, or it is a case that is a bit complicated, and you are not really sure what you will do next with it. And so you move that file from the center of your desk over to the side—left-hand side or right-hand side, it doesn't matter. You just want to get it out of your line of sight for the time being. But, lo and behold, you notice as you look around your office from time to time you can still see the darned thing—and it still makes your stomach tighten up. So you decide to move it behind you, to the credenza. You put a few other files on top of it. Finally, you get adept at sweeping your eyes around your office and not seeing that file at all.

In a perfect world, you could forget about that case completely. In reality, however, in most good firms someone is watching the computer printouts, and they may come in to remind you about the case. They may even ask you, "By the way, when were you thinking of billing on that case?"

What do most of us do when that happens?

We lie. We say something like, "Oh. Right. I was, in fact, thinking about doing that very soon. I'm just waiting for some disbursements to come in from Tasmania. As soon as those have arrived then I'll be ready to bill the thing."

Fear of Success

Many professionals have a fear of success.

That may sound preposterous to you. Why would anyone have a fear of success? Well, look at your own career. Have you ever had an opportunity to make a proposal to a significant prospective client and found yourself choking up—not knowing how to take the next step? Have you ever met someone who might be incredibly important to you and found the meeting awkward—found yourself incapable of performing to your best level?

What is that about?

Fear of success is a psychological problem many of us have, obviously without intending to, and it can get in the way of our progress. If you find yourself in situations like the one I have described, pause and break down the actions that you need to take into their component parts, and work very hard to avoid procrastinating. If the problem persists, you might want to consider doing some research into the fear-of-success syndrome and/or procrastination, or even getting professional coaching or other assistance in managing counter-productive patterns of behavior.

Managing Our Mental Blocks

There are a couple of approaches we can take to a mental-block case that can be very helpful. They are also quite simple. One was developed by the managing partner of a very successful, very prominent firm who was working on a matter involving a dispute over an estate on which he simply couldn't get himself to focus adequate attention. The deceased had been gone for some several years—in fact, the way the lawyer put it was, "When the beneficiaries started dying, I began to worry." He did not know what to do. He was traumatized by this case. So what he says he did was to go to a very junior lawyer, kneel down before her and clasp his hands together. He said, "Please, please help me with this case. The beneficiaries are dying. I have no idea what to do next. You're new. You've just been to law school. Maybe you will have some suggestions."

The young lawyer took the file away for a while, looked through it, identified some issues, and brought back a preliminary plan of action. The managing partner describes that as a life-saving experience.

Perhaps you find the concept of taking a sophisticated, difficult, complex case and giving it to the newest lawyer in the office a little extreme. But it is worthwhile to consider how fresh eyes, even new eyes, can sometimes see through the problems in mental-block cases with which we can no longer deal.

A second, related strategy is to trade mental-block cases—yes, trade them!—with a colleague, or a friend within the firm or, if you are a sole practitioner, maybe with a friend in a different firm, or another sole practitioner. The outcome of trading cases is almost magical. My mental-block case is not your mental-block case, and your mental-block case is not mine, and it is truly amazing how a fresh approach can cut through problems.

The Quiet Hour

As you have undoubtedly observed, you can get a lot more work done when the phone is not ringing, clients and colleagues are not running in and out of your office, and support staff are not continually asking for your guidance. As a result, many good lawyers fall by default into a time schedule where they arrive at the office extremely early in the morning, or they stay late into the evening. If that strategy works for you and gives you quality time to dedicate to challenging situations, then it may be a good approach in your case. However, it can also be a trap, because it can lead to your life being consumed completely by your practice. You can end up wasting an enormous amount of time as the day progresses, then working a lot of evenings, a lot of early mornings, and a lot of weekends. Before long your family members are wondering if you remember their names.

Alec Mackenzie, who wrote the internationally acclaimed book *The Time Trap*, makes a suggestion that he calls "the quiet hour." Simply put, the quiet hour is one hour, scheduled every day, that is dedicated to your concentration on a case or a matter that deserves your attention. You are unavailable for anything else during that time period, and you broadcast that fact to those with whom you work. Some people who use this strategy will even hang a sign outside their door indicating that they are progressing through a quiet time or quiet hour.

In employing this technique, you will need to recognize that you are going to build some tension with those with whom you work: they are going to come to see you and find that they have no access. Similarly, clients who call you may be irritated to be told that you are unavailable until the end of the hour. This means there is a pressure on you to be highly responsive when that hour is over. Your first priority at the end of your quiet time must be to get back to those staff members and clients who have tried to communicate with you while you were working in solitude.

A quiet time can convert an otherwise low-value hour during the day to a high-value hour. It is a strategy that may assist you in reducing the number of evening, morning, and weekend hours you need to spend in the office.

Making a Prioritized List

There is a story that is told to most business-school students about a consultant who was serving one of the Robber Barons involved in the steel industry in the early twentieth century. The Robber Baron, who happened to be huge in the steel industry, said that he wanted to improve efficiency and productivity, and he asked the consultant how they could do that.

The consultant gave him some advice, which could be reduced to a paragraph, and for that he apparently was paid $25,000—an enormous sum back in the early 1900s.

In essence, the consultant said, "At the beginning of every day make a to-do list of everything you want to accomplish. Put down on that list everything you want to achieve that day. Then, beside every item that is urgent on the list, place a U. Beside every item that is important, place an I. Now number these items. Begin numbering with those items that have both a U and an I, then go to those which have only an I and then finally number those which have only a U. Number them sequentially. Now start working. Begin with number one and don't leave number one until you are finished. If you are distracted unavoidably and taken to something else, then return to number one when the digression is finished. Work through those numbers in this manner until you are done."

One lesson to be learned from this story is to set priorities. As human beings we tend to have some less-than-productive habits. For example, if we have a number of things to accomplish, some of which are more fun than others, and we are operating in a loose or unstructured fashion, we may tend to go first to the items that might be more enjoyable.

A second lesson is not to be intimidated by the urgent. Most of us think that if something is urgent, we simply have to get at it very quickly. That is absolutely wrong. In fact, "important" should win out over "urgent" every time. Let me give you an example to illustrate this point.

Imagine that you are having a meeting with a prospective client. The client is the chief executive officer of a major corporation in an industry you would love to serve, and you are having a serious discussion about the possibility of your being retained. Your car is at a meter outside. It is approaching 4 P.M., and at 4 P.M. any car left there will be towed away. So what do you do?

Well, in spite of all the downsides, I think that most of us would say, "To heck with the car." If there is someone to run down and move it for you, fine, but if you have a choice between finishing the meeting with a prospective client that might enhance your satisfaction from your practice for the next decade or two, not to mention your income, or to avoid getting a ticket or having a car towed, I think you know which decision you would make. That is always the basis of the decision that needs to be made between the "I" and the "U," between the important and the urgent.

Every legal practitioner occasionally ought to look at the latest "time management" publications—read them, assimilate them, and put whatever useful information is within them to work. I suggest that you

---

Implementing Effective Strategies

The use of lists and priorities is one of those areas where "knowing" is not the same as "doing." You may right now be assimilating the information presented in this chapter about prioritizing the important and the urgent, and thinking, "Yes, that makes sense. Yes, I must try that some day."

If you are thinking in those terms, reflect for a moment on the difference between winners and losers. Winners look very carefully for those ideas which they think would actually have a high yield for them—then they implement those ideas.

If you do not think prioritized lists would be productive for you, then move on to the next idea. However, if you do think that this strategy would be of benefit to you, if you do think such lists would help you to use your time each day more effectively, then grab that pad and paper immediately and start making your lists, labeling the items with an "I" and a "U," and then assigning numbers to them. If you follow this methodology, you will find yourself getting a lot more done in the same amount of time.

---

take a moment now to identify one time-management tactic that might have an immediate positive impact on your practice—you choose which one it is. You will feel better knowing that you have started, no matter how small the first step is.

Whatever time-management tactics you deploy, whatever additional reading you do to learn about new ideas in this area, I promise you this—you will be emulating the best professionals in the world, and following their best practices. Such individuals continually look for ways to make their time more effective.

Chapter 47

The Power of Saying "No"

In most of the cultures on this planet, it is not polite—nor is it easy—to say "no." In fact, in most cultures, saying "no" is considered inappropriate behavior. As a result, due to our backgrounds most of us find it very difficult to say "no" when we have to, or when we should, in business or professional situations. However, we do ourselves no justice, nor do we serve our clients well, nor do we serve those with whom we practice well, if we say "yes" to everything.

People who say "yes" and take on too much simply fail to perform to expectation. We are far better off to be selective about what we undertake, but to always perform to expectation.

Saying "No"

In a lecture I attended, Alec Mackenzie, author of the book *The Time Trap,* focused on the art of saying "no." His is not the only system, but it is a good one.

Mackenzie's approach consists of five steps. The first is to *listen carefully* in order to understand the request that is being made of you. There is nothing worse than saying "no" to something you do not understand. Paraphrase or provide feedback if necessary, saying for example, "Let me just make sure I understand. You want me to prepare the document by Thursday at noon. Is my understanding correct?" Make sure you have it right.

The second step is to *say "no"*—politely but firmly. You will note that you do this before giving any explanation. Your "no" might sound something like this: "No. Candidly, I am not able to produce the document by Thursday at noon."

Step three is to *offer an explanation*—explain why you cannot fulfill the request. Say, "I would be unable to fulfill the other obligations I've undertaken and also prepare that document by Thursday. I would have to renege on another promise I made, and I am unable to do that."

The fourth step is to *offer assistance* or alternative solutions that will allow the person who made the request to accomplish his or her mission. In this way you will show that you are willing to assist as best you can, even though you are unable to say "yes" to the request. Say, for example, "Would it be of help to you if I looked around to see if there was anyone else available who could help you get that document done on your time frame?" Or, "Is it possible that you could manage the client's expectations so that I could do that document by Friday instead of by Thursday?"

The fifth and final step is to politely *admonish* the person who made the request. (This one really threw me for a loop when I first heard it. Admonish? I mean, normally we are talking about a client, or we are talking about someone who may be superior or senior to us in the firm. "Yes," Mackenzie says. "Admonish.") Your intent is to give a little bit of corrective feedback that might help the person making the request avoid getting into this kind of situation with you again in the future. You say something like, "Gee, I wish I had known about this when you first learned that you might need this document, because at that point in time I might have been able to schedule it in and get this done for you." Or, "In situations where you think I may be able to help in the future, let me know as soon as possible, and I'll clear the decks and see what I can do to help."

Those are Alec Mackenzie's five steps for saying "no." Given some practice, they can serve you well.

Chapter 48

Exploiting Opportunities

Over the course of this book, we have talked about many areas where you have planned and made decisions. You have decided what you want as your destiny and your future. You have thought about your preferred clientele, your preferred practice areas, and the industries with which you would prefer to work. You have considered tactics to help you achieve those goals. You have explored skills that will help you enhance client satisfaction, and attract new clients at will.

Before we conclude, it is important to touch on another phenomenon that occurs within the practice of law—as it does in all areas of our lives—and that is the unexpected opportunity. All of us need to be ready for such opportunities, and we need to have a mind-set that will allow us to properly embrace them.

Let me give you an example of an incident that ultimately provided a very important, even pivotal, moment in my practicing lifetime.

I started my law practice with an old, established firm of great lawyers. While I was still fairly junior, one of the clients I was allowed to participate in serving was a very significant corporation with huge revenues. Keeping this client happy meant a lot to the firm in terms of our potential future.

In Canada at that time, securities work was almost completely reserved for those few firms dealing with that area as a specialty—boutique firms, as we sometimes refer to them—and at that time our law firm did not do that kind of work. One day, one of the firm's partners came into my office and said, "Gerry, Client X needs some securities work. They are going to put their shares on the stock exchange. Who do you think we should refer them to?"

There were three firms in town that were extraordinarily good in that kind of work, and in fact, I had a good friend at one of them who I thought could do a superb job. So the easy answer would have been, "We could suggest Firm A or B or C—and I have a friend at C, so why not C?"

I did not do that. Instead I asked the partner, "Why can't we do that work?"

"Well, Gerry," he reminded me. "We don't have expertise in the area. We're not a boutique; we're not specialized. This is very sophisticated work. We wouldn't want to do anything less than the best quality work for Client X, would we?"

I agreed with him, but then I went on to argue, "I have friends who are experts in the area—friends in tax boutiques, friends in securities boutiques, friends who I could employ to work with me, to be on a team with me, to make sure that the work we did for this client was top of the curve in terms of quality."

He paused. Then he said, "Well, I suppose if the client agreed. . . ."

So we put it to the client—and we were very upfront about it. We explained that we were not a boutique, that we were not a specialist firm in the area they required. We explained, however, that we knew people who were. We reminded them that we knew a lot about their background because we had been serving them for a long time. We also suggested that perhaps we could hire and supervise those specialists more effectively than they could themselves directly.

They liked that idea a lot. In fact, they liked it enough that they were quite delighted to pay us a fee in addition to the fees that were going to the specialist. As it turned out, the total fee they paid was probably less than they might have paid to one of those boutiques had they approached them directly, but that is not the most important part of the story. The most important part of the story is the client got what the client needed, which was unsurpassed quality in the area they required.

What did the firm get? Well, we got two very important things. We strengthened the existing relationship with our client. We also began to build securities expertise in a way that was safe and appropriate for the client—in which no one's interests were jeopardized.

Building on Knowledge Gaps

How many situations do you encounter where a client needs something that is highly specialized, and you think, "That's not something I really do. That is not an area I know too much about. The client would really best be served to be sent to so-and-so"? Have you ever considered acquiring the expertise for the client by acting as the client's broker? (By the way, if you have such expertise within your firm, I am not suggesting that you hoard the legal work. In such instances, by all means send the work down the hall, staying in touch as appropriate for the purpose of maintaining the client relationship. You can refer to Chapter 17, "Transferring Clients Within the Firm," for more information on this topic.)

There are other potential applications for the concept of acting as a client's broker. My experience involved an area of law, but the same strategy could be expanded to deploy other experts from other disciplines on behalf of clients when required—such as consultants, engineers, or architects. Why can we not take charge of formulating a team that will help the client to achieve what the client wants to achieve? If we have established a fundamental relationship where we understand the client, we understand the client's objectives, we understand the people involved with the client, we understand how the client communicates, and we really do know how to serve them, then why should we not offer that knowledge as an added value when we bring in experts from different disciplines?

In the world today, we are seeing many sophisticated professional-service firms evolve into what is being called "multidisciplinary practices." This is a trend that will clearly continue well into the future. If you practice in a firm which is restricted in a traditional way to the practice of law, I suggest you ask yourself whether you, independently or even within the context of such a firm, can still provide multidisciplinary professional services to your clients by brokering the appropriate people for them.

Ironically, if you are a sole practitioner you may be more amenable to this idea than if you are in a large multifaceted firm. You know that you need to stay within the course of the work with which you are comfortable rather than taking a risk on quality that might put the client at a disadvantage, or damage the client relationship. However, whether you are a member of a large firm or a sole practitioner, the point remains the same—in addition to looking for opportunities, creating opportunities, and executing upon those opportunities as part of your work towards fulfilling your goals for the future, you also need to be ready to encounter opportunities that come right out of the blue. You need to be positioned and have an open attitude for opportunities like that.

When such opportunities arise, ask yourself the following questions:

1. Can you make a contribution that will be of value to the client?
2. Can you do that without jeopardizing the quality that the client deserves?
3. Is there some long-term benefit to you or your firm of building a team that includes individuals either from other firms or from other disciplines? For example, will you learn something that will make you more valuable as a professional into the future?

If the answer to those questions is "yes," then I suggest you consider how you may exploit such unexpected opportunities. If you are a member of a multidisciplinary group, even informally, you may already have the contacts in place. If not, then you ought to think about creating or joining such a group.

Even if you are less than prepared when such opportunities arise, with a little creativity you can probably quickly create the network you need to take advantage of them honorably, and to the benefit of everyone involved.

Conclusion

I extend to you a warm and sincere appreciation for the effort you have expended in reading this book, and putting relevant points and principles from The Successful Lawyer program to work for yourself. By doing so, you have moved well on your way toward a more successful practice.

You may not have the opportunity to revisit the content of this book very soon, but I highly recommend that you maintain your journal and your action list. Your journal should be revisited and updated frequently, as within it lie the ideas that are fueling your competitive advantage. I promise you this—the winners, the professionals who follow best practices, those individuals never lose their lists. They never lose sight of the actions that they have established as important to the achievement of their goals.

If I can be of help to you, you may contact me directly via e-mail at Edge International (riskin@edge.ai). Please visit my Web site at **www .gerryriskin.com** for additional contact information. I would be delighted to do whatever I can. Thank you.

Gerald A. Riskin
Anguilla, British West Indies

Resources

Cialdini, Robert B., *Influence: The Psychology of Persuasion*, Quill Books, William Morrow & Company, 1984, revised 1993.

de Bono, Edward, *Lateral Thinking: Creativity Step by Step*, Penguin, 1991.

de Bono, Edward, *Six Thinking Hats: An Essential Approach to Business Management*, Penguin, 2001.

Durham, James A., and McMurray, Deborah, editors, *The Lawyer's Guide to Marketing Your Practice*, Second Edition, ABA Law Practice Management Section, 2003.

Ewalt, Henry W., *Through the Client's Eyes: New Approaches to Get Clients to Hire You Again and Again*, Second Edition, ABA Law Practice Management Section, 2002.

Hornsby, William E., *Marketing and Legal Ethics: The Boundaries of Promoting Legal Services*, Third Edition, ABA Law Practice Management Section, 2000.

Mackenzie, Alec, *The Time Trap, Third Edition: The Classic Book on Time Management*, Amacom Books (American Management Association), 1997.

Maister, David H., *Managing the Professional Service Firm*, Free Press Paperbacks, Simon & Schuster, 1997.

Maister, David H., *True Professionalism: The Courage to Care About Your People, Your Clients, and Your Career*, Simon & Schuster, 2000.

McKenna, Patrick and Riskin, Gerald A., *Herding Cats*. Institute of Best Practices, Canada, 1995.

McKenna, Patrick and Riskin, Gerald A., *Beyond Knowing*, Institute of Best Practices, Canada, 2000.

Morgan, J. Harris, and Foonberg, Jay G, *How to Draft Bills Clients Rush to Pay,* Second Edition, ABA Law Practice Management Section, 2003.

Randall, Kerry, *Effective Yellow Pages Advertising for Lawyers: The Complete Guide to Creating Winning Ads,* ABA Law Practice Management Section, 2002.

Riskin, Gerald A. and McKenna, Patrick, *Practice Development: Creating The Marketing Mindset,* Butterworths Canada, 1989.

Siskind, Gregory H., McMurray, Deborah, and Klau, Richard P., *The Lawyer's Guide to Marketing on the Internet,* Second Edition, ABA Law Practice Management Section, 2002.

Snyder, Theda C., *Women Rainmakers' Best Marketing Tips,* Second Edition, ABA Law Practice Management Section, 2003.

Weishar, Hollis Hatfield, and Smiley, Joyce K., *Marketing Success Stories: Conversations with Leading Lawyers,* Second Edition, ABA Law Practice Management Section, 2004.

Index

Selected Books from . . .
THE ABA LAW PRACTICE MANAGEMENT SECTION

Law Office Procedures Manual for Solos and Small Firms, Third Edition
By Demetrios Dimitriou
This newly revised edition provides you with everything you need to develop and compile a succinct, comprehensive procedures manual, geared toward the unique management issues of a solo or small firm. This step-by-step guide offers direction on setting policy and procedures for your firm, and provides sample language and documents, both in the text and on the accompanying CD-ROM, to allow for easy customization. Proper implementation of sound policies and procedures will help ensure your firm operates effectively, efficiently and productively, resulting in optimal delivery of legal services to your clients.

The Essential Formbook: Comprehensive Management Tools for Lawyers, Vols. I-IV
By Gary A. Munneke and Anthony E. Davis
Useful to all legal practitioners this series will help you establish profitable, affirmative client relationships while avoiding unnecessary risks. And, all the forms are available on accompanying discs, making it easy to modify them to match your specific needs.

Volume I, Part I, addresses **Partnership and Organizational Agreements**, providing information about law firm management structure models, ethics, and general counsel. **Part II—Client Intake and Fee Agreements—** walks you through the intake process, including how to effectively gather information on new clients, manage the client selection process, make judgments, and use engagement and nonengagement letters.

Volume II, Part I, discusses **Human Resources**, and covers the hiring process, training and development, compensation, and discipline and termination. **Part II** covers **Fees, Billing, and Collection** and includes information on measuring billing practices, hourly billing, pricing legal services, alternative fee agreements, engagement letters, and managing the billing process.

Volume III, Part I, covers **Calendar, Docket and File Management**, including document backup, retention, destruction, and security. **Part II** outlines **Law Firm Financial Analysis**, including financial analysis of risks that all law firms confront.

Volume IV, Part I addresses **Disaster Planning and Recovery**, and offers guidance on both planning for disaster and on recovery after such an event, including contributing to the disaster relief of others. **Part II** covers **Risk Management and Professional Liability Insurance** and examines in detail professional liability insurance for lawyers.

Winning Alternatives to the Billable Hour: Strategies That Work, Second Edition
Edited by James A. Calloway and Mark A. Robertson
Find out how to initiate and implement different billing methods that make sense for you and your client. You'll learn how to explain—clearly and persuasively—the economic and client service advantages in changing billing methods. You'll discover how to establish a win-win billing situation with your clients no matter which method you choose. Written for lawyers in firms of all sizes, this book provides valuable examples, practical tools, and tips throughout. The appendix contains useful forms and examples from lawyers who have actually implemented alternative billing methods at their firms.

How to Start and Build a Law Practice, Platinum Fifth Edition
By Jay G Foonberg
This classic ABA Bestseller—now completely updated—is the primary resource for starting your own firm. This acclaimed book covers all aspects of getting started, including finding clients, determining the right location, setting fees, buying office equipment, maintaining an ethical and responsible practice, maximizing available resources, upholding your standards, and marketing your practice, just to name a few. In addition, you'll find a business plan template, forms, checklists, sample letters, and much more. A must for any lawyer just starting out—or growing a solo practice.

The Lawyer's Guide to Marketing on the Internet, Second Edition
By Gregory Siskind, Deborah McMurray, and Richard P. Klau
The Internet is a critical component of every law firm marketing strategy—no matter where you are, how large your firm is, or the areas in which you practice. Used effectively, a younger, smaller firm can present an image just as sophisticated and impressive as a larger and more-established firm. You can reach potential new clients in remote areas, at any time, for minimal cost. As with any other promotional tactic, the use of the Internet needs to be thoughtfully integrated into your overall marketing strategy. *The Lawyer's Guide to Marketing on the Internet*, Second Edition, can show you how to effectively and efficiently market your law practice on the Internet.

The Lawyer's Guide to Fact Finding on the Internet, Second Edition
By Carole A. Levitt and Mark E. Rosch
Written especially for legal professionals, this revised and expanded edition is a complete, hands-on guide to the best sites, secrets, and shortcuts for conducting efficient research on the Web. Containing over 600 pages of information, with over 100 screen shots of specific Web sites, this resource is filled with practical tips and advice on using specific sites, alerting readers to quirks or hard-to-find information. What's more, user-friendly icons immediately identify free sites, free-with-registration sites, and pay sites. An accompanying CD-ROM includes the links contained in the book, indexed, so you can easily navigate to these cream-of-the-crop Web sites without typing URLs into your browser.

ABA LawPracticeManagementSection
MARKETING • MANAGEMENT • TECHNOLOGY • FINANCE

The Lawyer's Guide to Marketing Your Practice, Second Edition

Edited by James A. Durham and Deborah McMurray

This book is packed with practical ideas, innovative strategies, useful checklists, and sample marketing and action plans to help you implement a successful, multi-faceted, and profit-enhancing marketing plan for your firm. Organized into four sections, this illuminating resource covers: Developing Your Approach; Enhancing Your Image; Implementing Marketing Strategies; and Maintaining Your Program. Appendix materials include an instructive primer on market research to inform you on research methodologies that support the marketing of legal services. The accompanying CD-ROM contains a wealth of checklists, plans, and other sample reports, questionnaires, and templates—all designed to make implementing your marketing strategy as easy as possible!

Through the Client's Eyes: New Approaches to Get Clients to Hire You Again and Again, Second Edition

By Henry W. Ewalt

This edition covers every aspect of the lawyer-client relationship, giving sound advice and fresh ideas on how to develop and maintain excellent client relationships. Author and seasoned practitioner Henry Ewalt shares tips on building relationships and trust, uncovering some unlikely ways to make connections in addition to traditional methods. Marketing techniques including brochures, newsletters, client dinners, and sporting events are discussed. Other topics that are covered include client intake, client meetings, follow-up, dissemination of news, fee setting and collection, and other client issues.

The Lawyer's Guide to Creating Persuasive Computer Presentations, Second Edition

By Ann Brenden and John Goodhue

This book explains the advantages of computer presentation resources, how to use them, what they can do, and the legal issues involved in their use. You'll learn how to use computer presentations in the courtroom, during opening statements, direct examination, cross examination, closing arguments, appellate arguments and more. This revised second edition has been updated to include new chapters on hardware and software that is currently being used for digital displays, and all-new sections that walk the reader through beginning skills, and some advanced PowerPoint® techniques. Also included is a CD-ROM containing on-screen tutorials illustrating techniques such as animating text, insertion and configuration of text and images, and a full sample PowerPoint final argument complete with audio, and much more.

The Lawyer's Guide to Strategic Planning: Defining, Setting, and Achieving Your Firm's Goals

By Thomas C. Grella and Michael L. Hudkins

This practice-building resource can be your guide to planning dynamic strategic plans and implementing them at your firm. You'll learn about the strategic planning process and how to establish goals in key planning areas such as law firm governance, competition, opening a new office, financial management, technology, marketing and competitive intelligence, client development and retention, and more. The accompanying CD-ROM contains a wealth of sample plans, policies, and statements, as well as numerous questionnaires. If you're serious about improving the way your firm works, increasing productivity, making better decisions, and setting your firm on the right course, this book is the resource you need.

Collecting Your Fee: Getting Paid from Intake to Invoice

By Edward Poll

This practical and user-friendly guide provides you with proven strategies and sound advice that will make the process of collecting your fees simpler, easier, and more effective! This handy resource provides you with the framework around which to structure your collection efforts. You'll learn how you can streamline your billing and collection process by hiring the appropriate staff and drafting a bill that the client is motivated to pay. In addition, you'll benefit from the strategies to use when the client fails to pay the bill on time and what you need to do to get paid when all else fails. Also included is a CD-ROM with sample forms, letters, agreements, and more for you to customize to your own practice needs.

Marketing Success Stories: Conversations with Leading Lawyers

Edited by Hollis Hatfield Weishar and Joyce K. Smiley

This practice-building resource is an insightful collection of anecdotes on successful and creative marketing techniques used by lawyers and marketing professionals in a variety of practice settings. These stories of marketing strategies that paid off will inspire you to greater heights. You'll gain an inside look at how successful lawyers market themselves, their practice specialties and their firms. In addition to dozens of first-hand accounts of success stories from practitioners, you'll find advice from in-house counsel and others who give candid feedback on how strategic marketing influences their decision to hire a specific firm. Learn how to make new contacts, gain more repeat business, increase your visibility within the community, and learn many other action steps with this worthwhile addition to your law firm's marketing library.

30-Day Risk-Free Order Form
Call Today! 1-800-285-2221
Monday–Friday, 7:30 AM – 5:30 PM, Central Time

Qty	Title	LPM Price	Regular Price	Total
_____	Collecting Your Fee: Getting Paid From Intake to Invoice (5110490)	$ 69.95	$ 79.95	$_____
_____	The Essential Formbook, Volume I (5110424V1)	169.95	199.95	$_____
_____	The Essential Formbook, Volume II (5110424V2)	169.95	199.95	$_____
_____	The Essential Formbook, Volume III (5110424V3)	169.95	199.95	$_____
_____	The Essential Formbook, Volume IV (5110424V4)	169.95	199.95	$_____
_____	How to Start and Build a Law Practice, Platinum Fifth Edition (5110508)	57.95	69.95	$_____
_____	Law Office Procedures Manual for Solos and Small Firms, Third Edition (5110522)	69.95	79.95	$_____
_____	The Lawyer's Guide to Creating Persuasive Computer Presentations, Second Edition (5110530)	79.95	99.95	$_____
_____	The Lawyer's Guide to Fact Finding on the Internet, Second Edition (5110497)	69.95	79.95	$_____
_____	The Lawyer's Guide to Marketing Your Practice, Second Edition (5110500)	79.95	89.95	$_____
_____	The Lawyer's Guide to Marketing on the Internet, Second Edition (5110484)	69.95	79.95	$_____
_____	The Lawyer's Guide to Strategic Planning (5110520)	59.95	79.95	$_____
_____	Marketing Success Stories, Second Edition (5110511)	64.95	74.95	$_____
_____	Through the Client's Eyes, Second Edition (5110480)	69.95	79.95	$_____
_____	Winning Alternatives to the Billable Hour, Second Edition (5110483)	129.95	149.95	$_____

*Postage and Handling	
$10.00 to $24.99	$5.95
$25.00 to $49.99	$9.95
$50.00 to $99.99	$12.95
$100.00 to $349.99	$17.95
$350 to $499.99	$24.95

**Tax
DC residents add 5.75%
IL residents add 8.75%
MD residents add 5%

*Postage and Handling	$_____
**Tax	$_____
TOTAL	$_____

PAYMENT

❑ Check enclosed (to the ABA)

❑ Visa   ❑ MasterCard   ❑ American Express

_____
Account Number   Exp. Date   Signature

Name _____ Firm _____

Address _____

City _____ State _____ Zip _____

Phone Number _____ E-Mail Address _____

Note: E-Mail address is required if ordering the
The Lawyer's Guide to Fact Finding on the Internet
E-mail Newsletter (5110498)

Guarantee
If—for any reason—you are not satisfied with your purchase, you may
return it within 30 days of receipt for a complete refund of the price of the
book(s). No questions asked!

Mail: ABA Publication Orders, P.O. Box 10892, Chicago, Illinois 60610-0892
♦ Phone: 1-800-285-2221 ♦ FAX: 312-988-5568

E-Mail: abasvcctr@abanet.org ♦ Internet: http://www.lawpractice.org/catalog